GUIDE TO
BRIDGE

MINTY CLINCH

© Haynes Publishing 2020
Published May 2020

A CIP Catalogue record for this book
is available from the British Library.

ISBN: 978 1 78521 680 0

Library of Congress control no. 2019950533

Published by Haynes Publishing,
Sparkford, Yeovil, Somerset BA22 7JJ, UK
Tel: 01963 440635
Int. tel: +44 1963 440635
Website: www.haynes.com

Printed in Malaysia.

Bluffer's Guide®, Bluffer's® and Bluff Your Way®
are registered trademarks.

Series Editor: David Allsop.

CONTENTS

Mahatma Gandhi used bridge to illustrate the difference between karma (fate) and dharma (action): there's nothing you can do about the cards you're dealt, it's the way you handle them that determines whether you win or lose – in life as well as at the table.

ANYONE FOR BRIDGE?

When the call comes, should the bluffer's hand go up? If it does, be aware that the game of bridge is exasperating, confrontational, tricky and malicious. And profoundly addictive. As you will soon discover, learning everything you'd need to know to match your fellow obsessives would take more than one lifetime. On the other hand, implementing the bluffer's mantra – *it's not what you know, but what they think you know* – should guarantee you preening rights among your peers.

There are plenty of excellent books about learning bridge, but this guide has the higher purpose of convincing others that you play much better than you do. As an ill-prepared pretender is all too easily outmanoeuvred and exposed, you'll need some bare essentials. First up, a rudimentary knowledge of trick playing-card games – ideally whist, but Oh Hell will do. As holding your own in bridge circles is the starting point, this guide assumes a smattering of bridge, but astute bluffers will absorb much more as they seek to dominate the corridors of power. More importantly you'll need chutzpah, preferably in spades, because *brigistas (see* Glossary) are often ready and very able to call your bluff.

In any campaign, success depends on appreciating what you're up against. Bridge is a game of byzantine complexity, with impenetrable layers that baffle only to enslave. The game is governed by rules written by men – definitely men – of a mathematical bent from centuries past. They have no aptitude for clarity, no mercy on the English language. You will be confused, but don't let that discourage you. Others will be confused, in every sense a bonus from your perspective. The Bible insists on three virtues, faith, hope and charity, the last of which it says is the greatest. Don't expect to find it here. No one said bridge had to be fun. As any aficionado will tell you, often too frequently for your liking, this is serious stuff.

At the highest level, players have minds like steel traps. At the lowest, they'd struggle to shut their hens in at night. Victors versus victims is the tip of the iceberg on an intense psychological battlefield.

As in many activities, the lucky take bridge up young when learning is compulsory and memory at its sharpest. Sadly an age that places aerobics, hiking and zumba on the moral high ground of leisure activities reduces the chance of a rare but incalculable bonus: a bridge-playing family. Don't worry. Rising break up rates are most auspicious. When a lone parent needs a partner, the simplest solution is usually sitting opposite you at breakfast.

Bridge is a card game for four players seated round a table, ideally baize, preferably green, but blue and red are acceptable, essentially with no mirrors in anyone's sightline. At the highest level, players have minds like steel traps. At the lowest, they'd struggle to shut their hens in at night. Victors versus victims is the tip of the iceberg on an intense psychological battlefield. With over 3 million players in the UK and 220 million worldwide, bridge is all things to all card players. Don't take it from this player. 'Bridge is quite simply the best game man has ever devised.' So says Andrew Robson, Britain's estimable *numero uno* who, in any conversation involving a bluffer's playing credentials, must be someone with whom you are intimately acquainted. Over a card table, ideally.

Mahatma Gandhi used the game to fulfil a higher purpose of zen-like calm and spirituality. He learned it, along with violin and ballroom dancing, as a law student in Britain between 1888 and 1891. During a game, a woman in his foursome made a lascivious pass. With his wife back home, he was lonely and about to succumb to temptation, when the hand of God stopped him; he claimed it was the deity's first intervention. Back in India and busy engineering independence from British colonial rule, he enjoyed the occasional rubber. More importantly, he used the game to illustrate the difference between karma (fate) and dharma (action): there's nothing you can do about the cards you're dealt, it's the way you handle them that determines whether you win or lose – in life as well as at the table.

In the informal setting of the kitchen, your partner is as chancy as your hands. At the start, the player who draws the highest card is the dealer. He* sits across from the player with the second highest card, leaving the other two to team up. Wine is poured, play commences, rubbers are won and lost, epithets grow fouler, clothing scantier, whisky is poured, memories are lost. *Match of the Day* intervenes, husbands are invited to sleep in spare rooms. In the morning, no one can remember who won.

In the drawing room, the tone is more refined. After an immaculate light lunch and a glass of white burgundy, players take their places around a Georgian card table. Crown Derby coffee cups sit on occasional tables within reach. Again picking cards decides who should play with who, but a more sophisticated scoring system means that everyone switches partners after four hands. Three rotations later, when everyone has played with everyone else, scores are totted up and an individual winner declared. Then it's time for afternoon tea.

* Men dominate bridge in the upper echelons – yes, it's an unavoidable truism of the game – but there's minimal gender bias at other levels. In the interests of economy rather than inequality, this book uses he and him rather than he/she or him/her. At the tables, prejudices of many kinds live on, but banning women is never on the agenda: there are far too many of them/us for that.

There comes a point in these social interactions when the 'duplicate' dragon stirs. This is the fork in the road. One route leads to a normal life with occasional pleasant and relaxed play, the other to addiction and all-out war. Duplicate is the international format for competitive bridge, designed to produce winners from any number of contestants. At its English grass roots, it is run by the English Bridge Union (EBU): 54,000 members and 620 affiliated clubs. Joining a small one with a single weekly competition costs as little at £5 a year, membership of a larger one offering games for different standards throughout the week averages £20–40. Table money is usually under £5 per session. Bridge does not break the bank.

The bluffer's lowly entry into this quagmire will be confusing. Typically between six and twelve tables are set out in a space – a community hall, a church hall, a social club – by dedicated committee members. The space is deemed too cold in winter, too hot in summer: *duplicateers* are not shy when it comes to complaint.

Once seated, the rookie is confronted by a plastic board or wallet containing pre-dealt cards in north, south, east and west pockets. Players are often known by these points on the compass. Once the cards have been played, they rotate in one direction and the partnerships in the other. The same hands are played by different couples throughout the evening, the results are calculated in percentages, then published as a table on the club website. Supposedly this represents equal opportunities. To remain sane, you'd better believe it doesn't.

With no introductions, no hint of who's who, the tyro's evening passes in a blur of faces, hands mis-bid, cards misplayed. At the end, their name appears at the bottom of the leader board. They will never risk the humiliation again. They repeat this vehemently, grumpily, despairingly, because they know they'll be back next week, re-engaged in the eerie maelstrom of silent play. They look at the poker faces without recognition, they stumble awkwardly between tables with others seeking their next opponents, their attempts at interplay chat are ignored. These players are here for the bridge. Again they come last, but they no longer kid themselves they won't be back.

Two shots is all it takes. One more than heroin, but a lifetime addiction nonetheless. And that's where this short but definitive guide comes in. It sets out to conduct you through the main danger zones encountered in any discussion about your bridge obsession, and to equip you with a vocabulary and evasive technique that will minimise the risk of being rumbled as a bluffer. It will provide you with a few easy-to-learn hints and methods that will allow you to be accepted as a bridge player of rare ability and experience. But it will do more. It will give you the tools to impress legions of marvelling onlookers with your knowledge and advice without anyone discovering that, before reading it, you didn't know the difference between a rubber of bridge and a royal pontoon.

THE SET-UP

KITCHEN ESSENTIALS

Table, four chairs, two packs of cards (one at a pinch), scoring stuff: a complimentary biro from a bank or hotel and the back of a used envelope marked out in vertical columns with a horizontal line halfway down – otherwise known as the planet saving option. This is the moment for the bluffer's first nugget of wisdom, namely that cotton paper playing cards, originally Chinese, later Egyptian, are symbols of human energy: **clubs** for industrious peasants, **diamonds** for wealth-creating merchants, **hearts** for clergy working on inner purity and joy, and **spades** for noble warriors inciting conflict. And the highest of these shall be spades – what else?

Once the 'who will play with who' draw is completed, the cards are shuffled and cut to he who had the highest so he can fire the opening salvo. He deals clockwise, starting with the player on his left (the dealer-in-waiting); 52 cards later, everyone should have 13, though misdeals are more common than they should be, especially in the kitchen. Meanwhile, the dealer's partner shuffles the second pack and places it on his right. When it's time for the second round, the dealer-in-waiting passes the pack on his left to the ex-dealer on his right. He cuts, the deal begins. ...

Any flaw in this historic protocol causes chaos – guaranteed, as you can pretty much rely on an error every time – but it can't be abandoned because it eliminates card-sharping (allegedly anyway, though members of the Magic Circle will always find a way). Rubber bridge (*see* page 14) was devised as a gambling game, tedious and pointless if no money was wagered. This is the moment to recall Winston Churchill's homily, 'playing for more than you can afford to lose ... only then will you learn the game'. Though mansions are rarely lost in gaming clubs nowadays, 1p a 100 is still a familiar stake in the kitchen and no one would want that compromised by bent distribution.

Once everyone is comfortable with all that, the bluffer assesses the value of his hand, counting four for an ace, three for a king, two for a queen and one for a jack. The total points for a pack come to 40. Add value for balance: a suit with six or more cards is a positive, especially if it becomes trumps. In a suit contract, a void (no cards in a suit) or a singleton (one card in a suit) offer potential for taking extra tricks with trumps. In no-trump contracts, it is often a killer, especially when partner is weak in the same suit.

Preliminaries completed, everybody arranges their cards in suits and counts. If the dealer's add up to 12 or more, he makes an opening bid. If they don't, he says 'pass' and the auction, the contest to establish who plays the hand in what contract, moves on to the player on his left. And so on. If no one has enough points to open, the hand is annulled and re-dealt, but this is mercifully rare.

To bid, the bluffer must know the hierarchy of the suits: clubs (lowest), diamonds, hearts, spades, up to no trumps. Need to know also includes their values: tricks in minor suits (clubs and diamonds) are worth 20 each, in majors (hearts and spades) 30, in no trumps 40 for the first and 30 for the rest. Tricks are the currency of success and failure, claimed by the highest card in the played suit when not trumped. Trumps are the suit that wins the auction, provided it's not no trumps. Got it. ...??

The bidding establishes the 'contract' – a commitment to making 6 (the base figure) of the 13 tricks, plus the number above it promised at auction's end. For example, closing the bidding on 4 spades promises 10 tricks (6 + 4). A game requires 100 points, but only ones scored below the line – as in bid and made – count towards it. Pluses for overtricks and penalties to the opposition if you fail to make a contract are written above the line.

Making a 100-point game in one hit means calling and making five clubs or diamonds (11 tricks in total – the base 6 + 5), four hearts or spades (10 tricks, 6 + 4) or three no trumps (9 tricks, 6 + 3). When bid and made, grand slams (all 13 tricks) and small slams (12 tricks) earn shedloads of points. A successful part-score, say three clubs or two hearts, is worth 60 below the line. To complete the game in the next hand, that pair need only bid two of any suit or one no trump (40) to reach 100. Keeping an eye on the score may lead to underbidding good hands in the interests of winning games. Should a player with slam potential (20+ points) bid the bare necessity to secure the game cheaply or risk all on a slam that may be impossible to make? As there is no right answer, the bluffer can safely offer an opinion.

A rubber is the best of three games. The winners of the first game are vulnerable, meaning that the penalties for tricks they bid, but fail to make, count double – 100 instead of 50 each – above the line in the opposition column. All this is taken into account when the rubber is completed and the scores totted up: 700 points above the line for two games straight, 500 for two out of three. Then the pence are distributed. Or the guineas, by the velvet sackload in earlier times. Beginners may feel they'll be struggling with these figures over many pain-racked months, but read on and play on: rewardingly soon, they'll be totting up with the best. For a newcomer, this would be a good moment to enlist three slightly better-informed friends to an intro session over a couple of bottles of wine.

Such an evening might go like this.After supper and undue consideration, Hannah opens 1C (*ie* one club), then raises hands to heaven. 'No, that's not right. Do you mind if I change it?' Resigned nods. 'Well, er, 1NT'. Then, 'Sorry partner, it'll have to be 1C. That's my call.' Hamish, partner and husband, looks bemused. 'Must have 12 to 14 points,' he thinks, '2NT,' he says. Hannah responds with 3NT, opponents double. A club contract is an easy make, but 3NT spirals into three down doubled and vulnerable. Big minus score, big red face, 'You only had 10 points, mostly in clubs,' Hamish grumbles. After the ace went, I couldn't get back into your hand to play them.' All that cooking and the evening has lurched into marital decline; Hannah reflects that it can only get worse.

Rashly, she splashes a bottle of decent Chablis into four fresh glasses and play resumes. Gillian pulls out her king of trumps. Everyone sees it before she snatches it back. 'No, that's ridiculous. I'm sure to lose it if I play it now.' She replaces it with the two. A hint that knowing where key cards are makes bridge pretty futile falls on very deaf ears. Play continues. A few tricks later, Hamish cunningly arranges for Gillian's king of hearts to fall under his ace. Gillian swears indelicately, heatedly, as if it were someone else's fault. Paul, her partner, looks glum. He's well used to this.

Hamish spots empty glasses and unscrews the Chilean Cab Sav. As levels fall, voices rise and with them keen rivalry. 'I will win this auction no matter what', is an expensive bridge habit. And by no means uncommon, especially among those bored by a string of unbiddable hands. By the time the auction reaches an unattainable contract, Hamish is desperate not to play the cards, but Hannah has gone beyond recall. She might have to go to 7NT, but she won't be stopped. Paul and Gillian suspect this but either they're satisfied with their pound of flesh or they want to be asked back so they double rather than goading her to the max. Then they sit back and watch her fall on her sword.

PARLOUR GAMES

The seating is arranged – a cushion at the back, a window opened a crack, the dog excluded to prevent asthma reaction or sentimental diversion. Each player has a commercial version of the scoring layout, a leather booklet of forms with Harrods or Smythson printed on the cover, complete with slim silver or gold pencils, ideally with silk tassels. No pens, no sharpies: scores need to be adjustable at any time. The rival scoring columns are marked We and They at the top. Don't be deceived by surface *politesse:* confrontation beats fiercely in every cashmere-covered breast.

Nowadays the short format Chicago scoring system is more popular than rubber bridge in drawing rooms around the land. The bluffer should win respect for a throwaway reference to the Standard Club of Chicago that takes credit for introducing and naming it in the early 1960s. No rubbers. This game has four hands, with vulnerability – the risk of doubled penalties – designated in advance. In the first hand, both pairs are non vulnerable; in the second and the third, the pair that deals is vulnerable, in the fourth everyone is vulnerable. The players rotate for the second, third and fourth rounds until everyone has played with everyone else. Tot up and start again. At the end, there is an individual winner.

These lips are not bred to openly criticise their partner's bids. To speak of victory or defeat would be vulgar so the struggle moves stealthily through the ebb and flow of play. No one would dream of mentioning cheating but diamond solitaire rings and brooches with four leaf clovers are part of this natural order. Everyone has a heart, whether stone or marshmallow. Few drawing rooms are complete without gilt-framed mirrors. Anyone with good eyesight or strong glasses may reasonably be disappointed to find the ones in their sightlines only reveal their own cards.

THE DUPLICATE CAULDRON

Time to throw bidding boxes into the mix to avoid the distraction of hearing what others call. These plastic devices hold cards showing every possible bid, from 1C (the lowest) to 7NT (the highest), plus pass (green), double (red), redouble (blue), stop (red) and alert (blue). The first test is to open the bottom, take out the cards and place them in the right slots. Failure to clip the bottom back firmly results in a deluge of slippery cards. Once they're out of order, they take an age to reassemble. Be patient as clutzes fumble. Your time will come.

Duplicate bridge is eerily silent. The club designates which direction is north, not necessarily geographically. The dominant player sits there and takes control, making sure the right boards (usually 1–26/27 depending on the number of tables) required for the game plan announced by the Director (*see* Glossary) are correctly orientated before play.

North also keeps the score, with east confirming it after each hand. Luddite clubs favour the cheap but time-consuming method approved by founding fathers in the last century. Each board is accompanied by a 'traveller' (because it goes all round the room), a form on which north writes the result of the hand. This is meticulously folded – no peeking at rival calls or results before play – and awkwardly slotted under a strip of plastic in the base of the board. Pressing on the indicated spot should make this easy, but the travellers become increasingly dog-eared as the evening progresses.

The luckless honorary scorer will appeal for accurate recording and neat handwriting, but he doesn't expect compliance. Next morning, contestants log obsessively on to the club website, unable to concentrate on anything else until the results are posted. Who could blame the scorer for delaying proceedings: every dogsbody deserves his day.

Modern usage prefers Bridgemates, electronic devices connected to a computer that collates the results on the spot. That's in a perfect world when every north can operate the machine for several hours without making mistakes that are a nightmare to rectify. And one in which there are no backlash adjustments incurred by infringements to the rules.

When told to operate a Bridgemate sight unseen, the most astute of bluffers has run out of wriggle room. However bitter, there's no alternative to putting up your hand and asking how it works. No shame attached: it's quite simple, but not immediately obvious. When fellow contestants crane forward to see what percentage they got and what previous players bid – revealed at the end of every hand – the claustrophobia is alarming. Resist the temptation to say, 'Easy guys, it's only a game.'

DO SAY: *'Apologies, everyone. I'm a Bridgemate virgin. You'll have to help me here.*
DON'T SAY: *'Easy guys, it's only a game.'*

Whichever system the club favours, the results are listed in percentages. Over 70% is outstanding and a certain winner. Usually 60+ is good enough to top the table. The 50s are respectable, the 40s draining, the 30s diabolical. Lower than that it should not go, though occasionally, wrist-slittingly, it does. Membership of the English Bridge Union (automatically included as soon as you join a club) commands a handicap based on your results. The best in Britain is Andrew Robson with 72.90%.

Depending on the master plan, two, three or four boards are played against the same pair before the Director calls 'move when you can'. As his job is to retain momentum, this may come before play is finished. Wall-mounted shot clocks, recently introduced in the UK, allow 15 minutes for two boards, 22 minutes for three. The countdown is relentless so don't be sucker punched by an adversary starting an involved story about his kids' A level results. A rushed player is a bad player so he may be reducing your game time for his advantage. The more rubbish he is, the more likely this is. The bluffer cuts him off, even as his son is opening the A-starred envelope. No remorse: gamesmanship is 'soft' cheating.

The Director's moving call is the signal for most to rise and mill around. At the start of the session, players pick discs out of a green baize bag. Black equals north/south, red equals east/west. Or vice versa. A few lucky north/souths, including the Director and the partially abled, get to sit in the same seats all evening. Excellent for maintaining focus and keeping track of your drink. Everyone else moves in formations reminiscent of an eightsome reel performed by Americans at a New Year's Eve ceilidh in Dundee. You always follow the man in the check shirt. Detecting a draught, he puts his woolly on. Where is he now? You mill some more. When there's one seat left, it's yours.

TEAM TORMENT

Every self-respecting club torments its members with monthly four-man teams: north/south sit at the same table all evening while east/west rotate to play the other north/souths. Getting into a good team is like waiting to be picked for school games. Lots of scope for rejection and affront: the bluffer suffers in dignified silence. Named squads must be signed up for a year, with reserves on the bench in case of injury or bereavement. Maestros are recruited swiftly, the rest accept the best they can get or stay at home. Would you rather be first reserve on a winning team or a founder member of a losing one that guarantees monthly play? It's easy to make the wrong choice.

You'll wonder why your relatively relaxed club is suddenly full of sharp-eyed opportunists. Easy: team bridge is the favoured expert format, assessed as more challenging, enjoyable and skilled than pairs. Winning is more prestigious. Crossing counties at midnight in mid-January is a small price to pay.

Getting into a good team is like waiting to be picked for school games. Lots of scope for rejection and affront: the bluffer suffers in dignified silence.

Each session starts with a team huddle. Pairs are scored in Match Points: if you go down massively in one hand, absorb the zero and move on. You may be able to recoup later. Teams are scored in IMPS (International Match Points), a cumulative system where every hand counts in the end result. In pairs, making more overtricks than your opponents is the difference between mediocrity and triumph; in teams, making games is the route to the top of the leader board. At the end, scores are correlated to produce a combo plus or minus table. Blame and shame? It's in the pipeline – a team's minus score can easily top 80 IMPS and the breakdown reveals exactly who's responsible.

In area league matches, your club fields a team of eight, two north/souths and two east/wests. If you're north/south, you'll play all four opposing east/wests in the course of the evening. And vice versa. With a break for tea and home-made cake. You may be asked to bake it. As in many other grass roots sports, club teams range far afield to meet up with league adversaries. Don't expect to be selected for home matches, but an approach from a desperate organiser for a distant away fixture is imminent.

If you feel diversion is better than outright refusal, trawl the thought of catching up with The Camrose. Pregnant pause, not at the realisation that bridge can be watched on computer (Bridge Base Online website), but astonishment that there'd be anything you'd want to see. Flash the snippet that The Camrose is bridge's answer to Six Nations rugby: home internationals between England, Wales, Scotland, Northern Ireland and Ireland. It is named after the Welsh newspaper magnate, William Ewart Berry, 1st Viscount of Camrose, who donated the trophy in 1936 when he was proprietor of the *Daily Telegraph*. The tournament showed admirable enlightenment in the gender battle by introducing a distaff division in 1951, light years before women's rugby was allowed to blight the game's escutcheon.

GLOBAL GOLD

The International Olympic Committee (IOC) has accepted bridge (and chess) as mind sports, but not as yet Olympic ones. The excuse is timetable congestion, the rationale that stretching the mind is no way as Olympian as exercising the body. The nearest bridge has come to participation was a demonstration event in the afternoon lull between morning snow competitions and evening ice ones at the 2002 Salt Lake City Winter Games.

In the 2018 Asian Games, Indonesian bridge supremo Michael Bambang Hartono, used a sliver of his $11billion clove cigarette fortune to get bridge scheduled alongside board games, chess, go and xiangi; the 78-year-old was rewarded with a bronze medal.

The downside of recognition is drug testing on the whim of the World Anti-Doping Agency. Crisis time, 2019: Norwegian pro player Geir Helgemo tested positive for the testosterone steroid Lance Armstrong used to cheat his way to multiple Tour de France victories; Helgemo also tested positive for the infertility drug clomifene. No one thought the 49-year-old was using illegals to improve his bridge, but he was banned for 12 months anyway. Great timing: he was already spending six of them in prison for tax offences.

THE HONEY POT

No matter how grand, bridge tournaments don't carry much prize money. In the 1950s, a major American television channel analysed live games between grand masters and celebrities whenever it could recruit them. If card by card play was underwhelming then, it would be commercial suicide today. No TV deals, no big bucks, but bridge champions have to eat. Start-up clubs, branded teaching programmes, journalism, published manuals and flip charts turn a tidy profit, but being a gun for hire is where the real money lies.

Becoming a pro is an evolution through the clubs and tournaments rather than a set career path. Think SUN – Sociability, Unflappability, Nous. Many punters regularly pay a professional – decent but not necessarily a high flyer – £100–200 to partner them in a daytime duplicate session at a club like Andrew Robson's. We're not talking billionaires, just lawyers, doctors and executives with cash to buy a pro rather than risk a cock-up with a mate. Interested? Take your pick from pro-bridge.co.uk – you can check out their photos first.

Warren Buffett, America's investment supremo, is in the market too. 'We can afford to lose money – even a lot of money. But we can't afford to lose reputation – even a shred of reputation.' Although he didn't say this in a bridge context, he'd happily hire a world champion for a six-figure sum to play with him for a week in a prestigious American tournament. Given the Buffett global reputation for steeliness in financial judgement calls, it's hard to say who'd be getting the better deal.

Vanity hiring can be even more expensive. As with polo, a rich man who plays to win at international championships must buy pairings and partners with enough skill to carry him to the podium. The team that bears his name should have five members who are more skilful than he is. By tournament rules, every participant must play in 50% of the games; the more the sponsor minimises his own play, the better his team will do. A more certain route to victory is signing up six pros and standing down himself, but where's the fun in that?

COME DANCE WITH ME

'Good bridge is like good sex,' quipped Mae West. 'If you don't have a good partner, you'd better have a good hand.' How right she was, but how to find one? Bridge is never a game for singles. Partners come in all degrees of ability and outlook. Some ask what trumps are as they play the hand; usually a guarantee of an unsuccessful outcome. Others shamelessly pass the buck: those who sneer whenever things go pear-shaped can never be in the wrong. Others interject snappy comments about systems flouted, basics forgotten, conventions (*see* page 43) misunderstood. As bluffers are likely to commit all these crimes in the quest for perfect play, enjoying bridge means finding *co-equipiers* with manageable egos. And rejecting those without.

A wannabe might be ambushed by a viscountess wearing a shirt-waister in a floral pattern at the bar of a club posh enough to provide partners for solos. 'Here on your own?' she'd trumpet. You nod numbly. 'Then you will play with me,' she says, brooking no dissent. You nod dumbly. You might think you'd done well when you bring in the first game contract, but you'd be wrong. 'Those diamonds were good. You should have made two more tricks,' she rasps coldly. The rabbit quivers visibly in the headlights. Another hand played, another shortfall detected. The rabbit should approach the organiser, begging: 'You have to remove that woman's vice-like grip from my jugular.' The organiser nods resignedly as she assigns alternative partners. Not the first time.

> 'Good bridge is like good sex. If you don't have a good partner, you'd better have a good hand.'
>
> *Mae West*

Nor the last. As a solo on a bridge break in Surrey, you might be recruited by a desperate woman in the corridor. 'You have to make up our four,' she'd plead. At the table sits your octogenarian nemesis, arrogance undimmed by the passing decades. As she looks you up and down, her pitiless glare leaves no room for doubt: such a social minnow never rates recognition – even if, as in this case, you've spent an intervening week together in the Sudan. Then again bluffers learn from mistakes: don't join them if you can't beat them, but if you can, make sure you do.

As the name suggests, a bluffer wanting to play duplicate pairs in a local club – a *duplicateer* – must have a partner. No mercy involved: turn up on your own and you're already on your way home. Getting one who doesn't want to kill you – and vice versa – requires guile and luck. The odds may be improved by the offer of a lift, but return journeys can be recriminatory. A shared sense of humour is a godsend, but the duplicate deity doesn't hand out fun lightly.

> As with wedlock – the operative word is lock – partnerships start with hearts and diamonds and end with clubs and spades.

PARTNERSHIPS

As with wedlock – the operative word is lock – partnerships start with hearts and diamonds and end with clubs and spades. The bluffer can embrace monogamy, building a mutual understanding of the labyrinthine conventions and signals required for success. Or he can flirt shamelessly, ditching the dross and sucking up to the stars. This is more amusing but more likely to result in evenings sitting in front of your TV wondering where you went wrong. In advance of the free choice which he certainly won't be given, the bluffer should assess the field.

Strictly mathematical

Accountants are on to every card. They never forget a convention and bid with admirable precision. Things get bitter when you factor in intuition: the notion of winging it doesn't appear on a spread sheet. Each errant trick will be analysed in the post-mortem. Forgotten when you played the two of clubs? No one else has. The call to move to another table is the best hope of salvation.

Carefree abandon

Cavaliers bid recklessly. Discipline? Who needs it. Play right out there on the edge. Let slip the hint of a decent hand after your partner opens and you'll be playing 6NT with two aces out against you. If spirits run high, so do tempers. And exasperation levels. And the rest. Enjoy any available *joie de vivre* because the results will be tragic.

Artificial Intelligence

Roundheads are hard wired for victory. Blank eyes stare across the table. Hands make precise placements from bidding box and cards. Body language is rigidly controlled, chilly and ruthless. The robotic roundhead allows no hint of emotion, no damning hint of life. Intimidated? Have no fear. You'll soon be ditched for a better coder.

Free spirits

Although the pundits scorn it, natural bidders often punch above their weight. Keeping the frills to a few unforgettable basics minimises confusion, anxiety, panic. Eliminating 'Christ, I'm sure that calling the opponent's suit at the two level means something, but what on earth can it be?' is liberating. Use the freedom wisely and you'll be surprised how high you finish.

The guilt trip

If luck smiles, better players may adopt you as a mascot, not as a permanent fixture but on a regular club pairs night – first Thursday, second Tuesday – each month. That leaves you with the task of managing their expectations. They're used to doing well so you'll squirm when they don't. These are perfect partners, studiously polite, kind, understanding and helpful in adversity, but Catholics should beware: the inevitable sense of letting them down is hard to bear. The fear of losing them only makes it worse.

Wedded bliss

A. As many as 50% of the regulars are locked into partnerships by marriage vows. Half of these are based on an unbridgeable bridge animosity: the better player can never fulfil his potential because the lesser one can never find anyone else to play with. Across the table, a set jaw and outrage bravely borne confronts the *faux* jollity of one who'll face a bitter debrief on the way home. Welcome these combinations for the free gifts they bring, and the unintentional entertainment they provide.

B. The other kind of wedded partnership falls squarely into the dread zone. All their waking hours are spent devising personalised bidding systems. In fact it's very hard to imagine them enjoying anything else. Questioned about their artificial bids at the table, they answer without hesitation or repetition, but with considerable deviation. These 'explanations' are not meant to be understood and they aren't, but it's all legit so don't mention cheating. At the end of the evening, such couples top the table, and they're already working on their next bidding system.

Smart play: hang on to the concept that every bluffer can be double bluffed.

Man to man

Happy chappies share girth and the pints that fuel it, their festive bridge spirits boosted by the joyful knowledge that their wives are watching the *EastEnders* omnibus back home. Did their better halves ever play? Certainly not with them. If they did, they've long given up in favour of knitting, crochet, croquet: anything but bridge. Freed from swain-leash, their menfolk have as good a grasp of card play as they do of domestic dominance. Cheerful smiles suggest an element of bonhomie that conceals an iron will to win.

Man to mistress

Increasingly à la mode in a constantly re-partnered world. Spot him by his languid confidence in his immortal right to charm and prevail. Spot her by her chic apparel, immaculately coiffed hair and nervous giggle. If she makes disastrous errors, will he look elsewhere? Bridge club line-ups aren't known for offering strikingly better romantic options, but roaming eyes never sleep.

Girl to girl

More accurately woman to woman, but bridge harks way back to the days before bras were burned to liberate females from the need to be forever young. A very wide playing field ranges from titters and whispers to the fierce intensity of she who embraces 'Me Too'. Bluffers may easily be confused by fluffiness hiding steel or a scholarly mien hiding daffiness. Always remember that the female of the species can be deadlier than the male.

When divorce is inevitable

As it will be as soon as the partnership drops in the results tables. Every *duplicateer* believes that practice makes perfect. Their own practice that is. They play at different clubs every night of the week: certainly possible within a 20-mile radius of their home. They dip patronisingly into drawing rooms and kitchens at weekends. They're as much in thrall to baize as golfers are to fairways and greens, but they don't have to tramp about in mud, rain and undergrowth. They live in a perfect year-round bubble of self-satisfaction. But what if it bursts? Step one is obvious: blame your partner. Too slow, too reckless, too cautious, too pedantic, too boring, too often sitting across the table looking pained at perceived errors. Yours, not theirs.

The next step is separation. By text? Too cowardly. By phone? Too embarrassing. Face to face? Far too embarrassing. Why not duck it altogether? As all philanderers know, often to their cost, re-partnering without telling the incumbent carries a savage backlash.

George: 'Hi, Simon, would you like a game on Tuesday? Celine isn't here this week.'

Simon: Awkward pause: 'Sorry old chap, she's already asked me to play with her.'

George is mortified, affronted, vengeful. The story is all over the club and many others within days. Some will admire Celine for her instinctive understanding of the foxholes in the battlefield; others side with George, their support marred by pity rather than compassion. The terminally insecure can see it might be their turn next. No bluffer worth his salt would put himself in that category.

Whether you're the duper or the duped, a new partner is required, preferably a better one. The partner criteria devised by Irish writer, William Donald Hamilton McCullough in *Aces Made Easy** may help. He offers a three-part suitability test based on the following scoring: 0–10 for bridge nous, 0–2 for intelligence and 0–10 for dishonesty. And the most important of these is dishonesty. Find someone with a score of 8 for willingness to deviate from the straight and narrow with 8 for nous and you have the perfect partner in bridge crime. Intelligence is much overrated.

Alternatively you can ask the long-suffering secretary of your club to email your request to other members. 'George is looking for a partner for Tuesday.' No reply is mortifying, but the desperate may have no option but to take this route – and to team up with the equally desperate person who responds. Then again, there may be a brilliant surprise. On a whim, a good player seeking a spontaneous night out takes a chance on a rookie. With the right cards, the right breaks, the right gods on your side, you may get an outstanding result and be asked to play again. You are on the first step of the ladder until the rung breaks. Cue guilt trip which the bluffer must learn to ignore. Thick skin is essential here.

*Pp.14–15, Methuen, 1934.

True romance

Does bridge offer scope for life partnerships? For those who've vowed not to hook up with anyone less intelligent than they are, the answer is maybe. One 30-something influencer starts the life partner search with a game of bridge. That way she weeds out the total thickos before going through a charade of disastrous dates. She tests potential suitors in her living room: cards over snacks and a couple of bottles of wine are much cheaper than going out Dutch. What does it take to win her approval? 'Bridge is not a sex substitute; sex is a bridge substitute' is her credo: bluffing lotharios must sharpen their tactics along with their claws.

Once romance has beckoned, with its attendant married bliss, it'd be a mistake to assume that a bridge player who rarely sees his spouse in the evening is in the market for sexual adventure. In the glow of a grand slam called and made, illicit passion might flare. Given the right cards – stars? – it might progress. The odds on bidding the contract may be good, those on making the game less so. Moving in together, booking a wedding date, a bridge honeymoon in the Maldives? Don't cancel Tinder yet.

DO SAY: *'Hang on to the concept that every bluffer can be double bluffed.'*
DON'T SAY: *''Bridge is not a sex substitute; sex is a bridge substitute.'*

It is said that there are more ways to arrange a deck of cards than there are atoms on the planet.

ADVANCED CALCULUS

Enter the rookie nervously. 'What do you play?' his new partner asks on club pairs night. It's a fair question and this is no time to stammer 'What do you mean?' It is said that there are more ways to arrange a deck of cards than there are atoms on the planet. For the mathematically inclined, that's 8×10 to the power of 67 combinations for 52 cards; 8 followed by 67 zeros makes repetition virtually impossible so any hand you hold on any given deal is unique from the beginning of time. Or so some pundits insist, though it's hard to get your head around it. Then again, other maths geniuses say it's not true because the random effect of chance must be factored in.

The ultimate quirky hand – four 13-card suits – comes up more frequently than these odds suggest. A wobbly bluffer might foolishly remark that dealing a pack straight from the cellophane would produce this phenomenon. Wrong, unless a maverick manufacturer had sorted the deck numerically (four twos, four threes etc) rather than in suits, as is normal. A mischievous bluffer might substitute fixed cards for the ones in the board. And bid a grand slam in whichever suit he holds. Hang on: this is the moment to be very afraid. If your bid is allowed to stand, your 13-trump hand is a put down winner. When 7NT comes up, your cards are useless: he who leads takes all.

Charles Anderson-Pelham, 2nd Earl of Yarborough (1809–62) is a useful red herring when large numbers come up. As a dedicated Victorian whist gambler, he calculated the odds on getting 13 cards without aces, kings, queens, jacks or tens (collectively known as honours) are 1,400 to 1. Accordingly he announced a running bet: every time he had a hand with an honour, he'd receive £1; every time he had a hand with no honours, he'd pay out £1,000. Over the years, he accrued a small – or not so small – fortune. A hand with no card higher than a nine – useless in most circumstances – has been known as a yarborough ever since.

BIDDING SYSTEMS

Creating order out of chaos in bridge means picking a bidding system, sticking to it and making it work for you as a pair. Your partner is your best friend – though it may often seem otherwise – and picking the right contract together is a matter of give and take. The hog bids to play every hand himself, something he justifies by the sincere belief that no one could possibly do it better. The wimp bids – or fails to bid – with equal selfishness. Unless his cards are so good that the contract is guaranteed, he doesn't plan to play them so he skews the bidding to make sure he doesn't.

Both approaches miss the point of bidding, which is to trade information about your hands, ideally legally. Sticking to the basic system is relatively simple, but it's only the tip of the iceberg.

DO SAY: *'Your partner is your best friend – though it may often seem otherwise – but picking the right contract together requires serious give and take.'*

DON'T SAY: *'It's no use playing with a bridge pig who hogs the hands in the belief he can play them better. Or with a bridge wimp who passes on certainties in case he can't.'*

ACOL

Alone among major bridge-playing nations, Britain favours Acol, the bridge bidding system designed to be as natural as possible by originators, Jack Marx and 'Skid' Simon. Buffer's bonus for conjuring up images of the duo polishing their masterwork on long walks on leafy back streets in Swiss Cottage in the 1930s.

It takes its name from their starting point, the Acol Bridge Club, established in Acol Road (itself named after a Kent village) in West Hampstead, in 1930, by resident silk merchant, William Druiffe. As the club's first secretary, he advertised as follows in *The Times* on 24 March:

'Capable and experienced lady wanted to take charge of the bridge room of one of the newest and most enterprising bridge clubs of north west London. Applicants must have great personal charm, be quite alive, and have plenty of initiative, able to play a really first-class game of bridge and have a good following.'

The winner must have met the spec: the prestigious club plays on in premises it took over in 1946 in neighbouring West End Lane.

Although it can be used with the *strong no trump* (15–17) favoured in America and most bridge nations, Acol's lynchpin is the *weak no trump*: 12–14 points and a balanced hand (no more than five cards in the longest suit, no less than two in the shortest). !NT is a familiar opening: like any artificial bid, this must be flagged up to the opposition so partner announces, '12 to 14'. Cue number crunching and head scratching.

In duplicate, making a game requires a bid of 5C/5D, 4H/4S or 3NT. Success is rewarded with plus scores of 400 points for a game in 5C/5D or 3NT; and 420 for one in 4H/4S.

VULNERABILITY

The bluffer might grasp this in one easy lesson, but there are two complications that befuddle and bemuse. The first is vulnerability. This is predetermined for each hand and announced in red rather than green on the plastic card holder (board). When you're vulnerable and opponents aren't, your potential rewards and risks are greater. Making a game contract earns a 200-point bonus (600/620); failing costs double penalties (100 rather than 50) for every trick you promise and fail to make.

If opponents are vulnerable and you're not, your risks are cheaper so you can bid with more abandon. Sacrifice chat (*see* Glossary) indicates bluffer sophistication – not a live goat, but a bid for a contract you expect to lose that carries less penalties than the opponents' winning one. Of course the reveal may show opponents couldn't have made theirs anyway. Who's the goat now?

DOUBLE TROUBLE

The second twist is bridge's gauntlet: the double. The little red card with the white cross is a skull and crossbones: go here at your peril. By throwing it down at the end of bidding – as opposed to early on when it means one of several completely different things – the opponent says, 'Liar. There's no way you'll make that contract.' Doubled penalties are incremental – grievous when you're not vulnerable, irretrievably damaging when you are. An attempt at an escape bid may result in an even more impossible contract that will of course be doubled. The supreme double bluffer can flash the redouble card: blue with two white crosses signifying icy certainty. Pure funk would usually be more appropriate.

PLAYING THE ODDS

Bidding to win means taking account of the possible outcomes – basically playing the odds. The effective gamer displays enviable expertise by rattling off each hand's score before the Bridgemate chips in 'Mm, so that's seven no trumps vulnerable and doubled. I make that plus 2,490.' Step up, Pythagoras. It's only numbers.

GET TO THE POINTS

Believe it or not, you're now equipped to count your high card points (HCPs), assess your hand and get started. How many points can your partnership have? If you open 1NT (12–14) your partner will need at least 11 and possibly 13 to add up to 25 (out of 40), a realistic basis for a 3NT game. You'll need 33 for a 6NT small slam, 37 for a 7NT grand slam. Reality check: that's when the gods smile. What if partner* has zero to add to your 12–14 opener? The cheery bluffer responds to the disaster by recalling that others will play the same cards. A dilemma shared may be a dilemma halved. Or doubled.

If you don't have the points, the opponents do. In extremis, they're your lifeline, but only if they bid. In killer mood with strong cards, they will, but it'll be 'double', a potential penalty bonanza for them. Andrew Robson's favourite play is a tricky 1NT doubled and vulnerable, but he can work out where every card is. If you can't, it's unlikely to be yours. Minus 1,100 for four down doubled and vulnerable is a not unfamiliar disaster.

Even the humblest duplicate pairs hinge on convention cards (*see* Glossary). 'May I see your card?' comes right after 'what do you play?' in partner's initial quiz. No is the accurate answer – as in it doesn't exist. 'Would you help me here' is a better response than

---

* It is part of bridge etiquette not to precede 'partner' with 'your' or 'the'. This is a yawning elephant trap for bluffers. Take note.

'What's that?' He hands you his. You scan it cautiously. A weak jump overcall? An unassuming cue bid? A multi-two diamond?

As undecipherable as ancient Greek, but bluffers can't act baffled. 'Fine' is certainly a lie, probably a mistake, but it's far too late to question the inevitable carnage. Pick your first hand out of the slot with an insouciant smile, arrange cards in suits, count points. Let declarer bid, let fate decide.

Converts are the most ardent believers. So says the Catholic church, so says the newly addicted duplicateer.

THE BLAME GAME

CONVENTIONAL WISDOM

Conventions are an art form: you say what you don't mean so that partner can say what you do. Partner reaction to your failure to recognise and/or respond correctly ranges from resignation through indignation, infantile tantrums and blind fury to walking out on the spot. There are logical reasons for some of the complexities – if the weaker hand is tabled as dummy* (*see* pages 68/69), the partnership's strengths remain hidden. Others seem hostile, arbitrary, too complicated for their own good, too complicated for yours – or all of the above.

Converts are the most ardent believers. So says the Catholic church, so says the newly addicted *duplicateer*. By pairs week two at his club, he will be armed with the blank convention form downloaded from the English, Scottish, Welsh, Northern Irish or Irish Bridge Union

---

* Note that, as with 'partner', dummy is never preceded by 'the' or 'your'.

websites. Again he will be puzzled: so many alarmingly empty spaces; so little intel to fill them with. The details of the selected system seem pitifully meagre, so divert with selective name dropping. Be sparing, though: boring people to death is not the object here.

BENJI ACOL

In contemporary club duplicate, this is the system most people say they play. You should too. Conjure up Albert Benjamin, Glasgow-born to a Swedish father and a Siberian mother in 1909. He it was who noticed that some of the strong two opening bids that ruled at the time were underused. 2C meaning 23+ points (and not necessarily any clubs), was the accepted format for an outstanding hand, game forcing with slam potential, 2D, 2H and 2S, meaning six good cards and around 20 points, was a waste of bidding space because it occurred so rarely. As a true Scot, Albert deplored that. He *benjaminised* a weak two variant based on opening 2H or 2S with a six-card suit and 5–10 points. 2D indicates the top 23+ points, with 2C relegated to 19–20 points, either balanced or with eight playing tricks. The bluffer should also be aware of reverse – perverse? – Benji in which those two bids are switched, but only by previous agreement with partner. 2NT = 21–22 balanced. Bingo, you're good to go.

Pause a moment to take comfort from author Somerset Maugham. In 1934, he was asked by pundit, Charles Goren, to write an intro to his new *Standard Book on Bidding*. As an indifferent player, Maugham sensed an opportunity: 'Having a practical side to my otherwise idealistic nature, I told him I thought I should let him know at once what my terms were. He paled. They were that he should dine and play bridge with me. He heaved a sigh of relief and accepted.'

If you have a cool head, the ability to put two and two together and come up with the right answer, and if you will tell the exact truth about your hand, you will be a useful partner and a formidable opponent.'

W. Somerset Maugham

Having revelled in his bridge moment, Maugham turned to the quid pro quo. 'When I read the *Standard Book on Bidding*, I felt I could never remember all the rules it gave me and that to try to do so would only confuse me,' he wrote in his essay, *How I Like to Play Bridge*. 'Presently it dawned on me that very few, no more than half a dozen, obligatory rules must be followed, as with any game – and the rest is horse sense. If you have that and are prepared to abide by it, you need not clutter up your brain with other precepts. The moral was clear. If you have a cool head, the ability to put two and two together and come up with the right answer, and if you will tell the exact truth about your hand, you will be a useful partner and a formidable opponent.'

He goes on to say that although everyone should learn bridge, not everyone should play it: those with no card sense – in his opinion, a defect of nature like being colour blind or tone deaf – should choose solitaire instead.

STAYMAN

A 'must learn' system for establishing a four-card fit in the major suits. Opener calls 1NT. With 11+ points and a four-card major, partner responds 2C, asking if opener has spades or hearts. If he does, he names the suit and the race for the game is on. Thank Manhattan-based industrialist, Sam Stayman for this one. He didn't invent it – the Brits did – but his write-up in *Bridge World* in 1946 grabbed the glory.

NAMYATS

Not a tropical fruit, but Stayman spelled backwards to snare a convention involving transfers from 4C/4D openers into 4H/4S to indicate an exceptionally long/ strong major suit. What an ego! Fellow New Yorker, Victor Mitchell, claimed the same convention as the Mitchell Transfer. Bonus points for mentioning – perhaps imitating – his wife Jacqui, a fellow international who filled dull – or dummy – time by doing her embroidery. Commend home-bred resistance to ego-naming: in Blighty, Namyats is known as the South African Transfer.

JACOBY TRANSFER

Brooklyn-born Oswald Jacoby – known to his intimates as Ozzie or Jake – takes the credit for this essential switch system. The ability to multiply three and four digit numbers in his head led to a career as a spy during the Korean War and a lifetime of top-level bridge as player, author and journalist. To Americanise your reference, pronounce him JacOby. His transfer is well loved because it is unusually easy to learn and remember.

Over an opening 1NT, a partner with the appropriate five card major or six card minor calls 2D if he wants a transfer to 2H, 2H if he wants 2S, 2S if he wants 3C, 3C if he wants 3D.

This means the weaker hand goes down as dummy and the combination should have a lot of trumps, if not much else. The concept crops up regularly so it's never too early to grasp the nettle. Or to appreciate how swiftly it can sting. When you forget and fail to complete the transfer – as you will – partner is stranded in an unplayable contract. He may hate you for that. Few will blame him.

JACOBY 2NT

A strong bid over your opening 1H or 1S is a plea to aim high. Partner has at least 12 points and four cards in your suit. Time to go slamming? Or slam dunking? Slip in Leo Baron, the German-born, British-raised Second World War squadron leader who actually devised it. As a lawyer, he later worked with black nationalists to secure recognition for Zimbabwe, the country he adopted (as Southern Rhodesia) in 1952. Aspects of this admirable CV didn't appeal to Americans of the era and so they passed the bragging rights to good old Ozzie above.

OGUST

Thanks are due to Harold A. Ogust, the New Yorker responsible for a 2NT response to a weak 2H or 2S, followed by one of a sequence of bids that reveal the suit's strength. Foolproof? Yes, if you can grasp and execute seamlessly. You will of course add that this is also known as a Blue Club response, as promoted by Neapolitan global star, Benito Garozzo, in the 1960s.

FOURTH SUIT FORCING

No accreditation, but a 'must mention' for its popularity and ability to create irreversibly hostile contracts. As the name implies, it's an invitation to play no trumps when three suits are confirmed, the fourth in doubt. He who calls it promises half a stop in the unbid suit. What exactly is that? All you need to know is – get it wrong, and you're dog meat.

LENGTH IS STRENGTH

Not a convention per se, but devices for revealing two long card suits to find a fit over opponent's opener. Sorting out the multiple ways of identifying them demands prodigious memory and clear thinking. Step one is to spot the convention. Step two is to whip out that blue Alert card and wave it in front of the opponents. If you don't, the wily may leave it be: asking you what your partner means, as they're entitled to do, warns you that you've screwed up. If they do ask, you've a couple of seconds to dredge up the correct response. Use them wisely. If not, 'We're a new partnership so we haven't really discussed that,' works once or twice.

GAME AIM

You need to share your 5/4 and 5/5 suit combos with your partner as efficiently and cheaply as possible. Here's what you must claim to know about:

1. Overcalls over opponent's opening 1NT
a. Landy
   A 2C overcall denotes 5/4 (ideally 5/5) in the majors and a minimum 8 points. Alvin Landy from Ohio came up with that one.
b. Multi Landy
   A more complex version that is moving towards world domination. 2C = 5/4 in the majors, 2D = an unidentified six-card major, = 2H or 2S = 4/5 cards in the stated major and an unidentified minor, 2NT = 5/5 in both minors. Provided your partner has recognised these possibilities, he'll know precisely what to bid next ... if he hasn't or doesn't, you're toast. Badly burned.
c. Cappelletti/Pottage/Hamilton
   Inevitably there were those who thought they could

add micro-variants to hijack Landy's glory. You can confidently name Armand Michael Cappelletti, son of a Rhode Island carpenter, lawyer to government greats in Washington DC; John Pottage, Andrew Robson's partner in victory in the Junior World Championship in 1989; Fred Hamilton, Michigan-born world champion and Grand Master. Almost anyone else. ...

2. Overcalls over opponent's opening suit.

a. Michaels Cue Bid

Step up Michael Michaels from Miami Beach. His brainchild is as repetitious as his name: calling opponent's opening suit at the next level shows two five-card suits: *eg* 1C from opponents, 2C from your partner. Odd enough to be a wake-up call, but complications escalate. If the opener's suit is a minor, the Michaels caller should have five in both majors. If it's a major, he needs five in the other major and an unidentified minor. Super Michaels, Modified Michaels and Leaping Michaels add lustre. The bluffer can add obfuscation with a reference to the Muiderberg Convention, favoured by the Dutch, but known as Lucas Two or Woo Two in other parts.

b. The Unassuming Cue Bid

So unassuming that it remains unclaimed in the pantheon of fame. Repeat opener's suit at the next level (with 10+ points) after partner calls a five-card major to show potential for game for even slam.

Not to be confused with the Unusual No Trump, a first-round 2NT overcall that declares five cards in the two lowest unbid suits. Ah well. ...

c. **Ghestem aka CRO**

Pierre Ghestem from Lille came up with this one; it's so Delphic that the Americans left it with him, but it's the most precise way of saying exactly which two five-card suits you have in a single overcall. Priceless if only you could remember it. Your first leap in the dark may take you straight to 2NT or 3C over opponent's one-level opener, already very high and easily confused with other 2NT conventions such as the Unusual. Partner responds according to a code involving pointys – diamonds and spades – and roundys – clubs and hearts. CRO does the same job in a different way. It stands for **colour**, **rank** and **odd**. Throwing in **Raptor** ('wRAP around TORonto style'), which is credited to Canada but evolved in Poland and Sweden, should impress, though it's hard to say who. ...

RED ALERT

A different partner means a different convention card so expect a tricky preamble, as in 'Do you play (any of the above)?' Once Benji Acol is agreed, Stayman and red transfers are pretty much automatic. Some partners will only open five-card majors; if you haven't got one, it's 1C or 1D with a minimum of three cards and an agreement as to what comes next.

Bids reveal how strong your hand is, but usually you need more than one to paint the full picture. If no one else has opened and you have 12 points, try to find a call, however unpromising. The rule of 20 (number of cards in two suits + points totalling 20) may allow a

10- or 11-point opener. A weak responder (5 to 9 points) repeats the suit at the two level with three-card support. If he passes the rule of 14 (number of cards in longest suit + points totalling 14), he switches to his suit at the two level. If you open 1NT (12–14), partner passes with 10 or less, unless he has a five-card major to trigger a transfer. With 11+ and a four-card major, it's Stayman.

Factor in relay bids (ploys for requesting more info), pre-emptive threes and fours (weak openings with seven- or eight-card suits) and jump overcalls. Ride the convention merry-go-round. Has your partner captured or forgotten the prescribed response? Is the opposition nipping in to spoil or sacrifice or play a hand rather than do their embroidery?

Is this the moment to slip in a 'psych' (*see* Glossary), a bid so outrageously misleading that all around you sit with mouths agape. You might expect this to be illegal in the convention-driven bubble, but you'd be wrong. There are two caveats: partner must be as ignorant as the opponents so it can't be part of your system and it must be used very sparingly. A repeated pattern can be construed as reinventing your system without telling the opposition, a heinous crime. After all this, the bidding has probably gone too high for anyone to make any kind of contract. Damage limitation? Far, far too late.

THE BIG TIME

Throw in RKCB as soon as you can because the thought of a slam cheers everyone up. In most circles, including kitchen and parlour, **Roman Key Card Blackwood** (you'll know it's named for the famous 1960s Italian Blue Team) has replaced **Standard Blackwood,** named for Alabama-born Easley Rutland Blackwood, as the preferred golden gun. After a bidding sequence with slam potential, 4NT asks how many of the five key cards (four aces/king of trumps) partner has. 5C = 0 or three, 5D = one or four, 5H = two and no queen of trumps, 5S + two + queen of trumps. 5NT asks for kings, omitted except when contemplating a grand slam because replies at the six level are already past most points of no return. In the interests of seizing complexity out of simplicity, partner may prefer the 1430 variant which reverses the 5C/5D values. 'Are you 3014 or 1430?', not BC or AD, but a must ask at the outset or that glorious slam moment will be blown out of the water.

The glitz may escalate, but opponents must not vegetate. Rather they should slip in a **Lightner lead-directing double** – thank you Teddy from Michigan for that one. Doubling a slam asks for an unusual lead. Identify the void or other pitfall correctly and the contract is doomed. Oh dear.

7NT is the prize of prizes. 'Most of the people in this room would never bid it', a cocky opponent might say sneeringly. No L-plate bluffer would sink so low. If the numbers stack up and your luck is in, the egg will be on his face. If they don't, it's a zero, but there are always plenty of those.

ß

You may feel you're awaiting sentencing by a hostile jury. As you are. Many a player is psyched out of a club by the dawning certainty that no one wants them in it. Don't let the 'always one' theory of group dynamics upset your equilibrium.

THE MIND GAME

Most things you do at the bridge table can be analysed and used against you. Walk into the room with assumed confidence, careful not to catch anyone's eye. These strangers aren't looking to meet and greet, especially not upstart invaders from another planet. But they'd sure like to assess your vulnerabilities. Find partner, pick empty seat, wait. Beware choosing north: he has to operate the Bridgemate or write down the score. There's no value in revealing incompetence: under the radar is the safer option.

DRESS MATTERS

Of course dress matters. If you wouldn't necessarily think so when reviewing a roomful of *duplicateers*, that's because you're wilfully blind.

For him

As a rule of thumb, the more crumpled you are the better you should play; the bluffer should leave his Armani in the wardrobe. At local level, the male tone is casual, ranging from well-worn polo shirts on singles to neatly pressed check shirts on males with wives that iron. Obesity is often a badge of expertise: that straining belt under the belly doesn't suggest time wasting on outdoor pursuits. Colours are muted. Hair is much as it grows – or doesn't. For a forbidding aspect, try bare feet in sandals with shorts in midwinter, but only if you're tough enough to survive in a draughty hall. Blue is not appealing, A & E less so.

For her
Ladies aim for comfort rather than cocktails, but they look much fitter, usually from doing the garden or walking the dog. Many have hairstyles and necklaces or scarves to jazz up skirts and blouses. On the principle that battle paint is a weapon, some wear full make- up. Their war may not involve cards. With a selection of single or *faux* single men, bridge rooms are viewed as an opportunity. Smile into partner's eyes over 27 hands and he may be yours. Or off your list forever.

TABLE MANNERS

At your chosen table, the first opponents take the other seats, meticulously determined not to introduce themselves, faces set. You may feel you're awaiting sentencing by a hostile jury. As you are. Many a player is psyched out of a club by the dawning certainty that no one wants them in it. Don't let the 'always one' theory of group dynamics upset your equilibrium. The notion that 'if no one else is the fall guy, it must be you' may be correct, but this is no time for paranoia. Hang in there; play will commence.

LATE ARRIVALS

That's after late arrivals have ruined the original game plan, always dependent on how many couples turn up. Another table must be erected, more bidding boxes set out, a spare Bridgemate booted up. The Director looks resigned as he collects the original movement cards, renumbers the tables and selects a scheme that incorporates the new arrivals. By the time he's sorted it, he can barely bring himself to say, 'Enjoy your bridge.' As he must, as he does through gritted teeth. Cue for everyone to grab their cards.

SLEIGHT OF HAND

The astute bluffer takes it more slowly. Counting cards face down before you look at them is irritating and usually pointless, but essential for the expertise it suggests. Arrange cards in suits, tot up points, groan inwardly. For experts, body language, theirs and yours, is a work in progress. Consistency earns respect so pick out the card you want to play and lay it smoothly on the table. When the trick's done, place your card vertically if it's a winner, horizontally if it's a loser, in a neat line in front of you. Dummy should also do this, however tedious. At the end of the hand, there may be arguments over who's won what. An accurate line-up is the only way of sorting out hostilities.

REPETITION

Repeat the same movements every time, regardless of whether you're scoring with an ace or discarding a two. Don't fidget or lean back irritably or chuck useless cards down with a scowl. Don't roll your eyes in alarm or despair. Don't pull out a card ahead of your turn: waving it in the air might indicate a singleton, vital ammo to the oppo, especially if it's the last trump. Note how experts do it: don't be out-bluffed.

ALL CHANGE

After two, three or four boards, it's time to change opponents. This may leave a significant gap while others finish up after the Director, always keen to beat the clock, has shouted 'Move when you can.' To talk or not to talk. Going through the mistakes you've made or the irritations partner has caused you are popular topics, but not usually positive for your prospects. Gloating, should there be any cause, is odious. Instead the bluffer might assess opponents for an idiot ice-breaker. Avoid the one who looks as if he squirmed out of the birth canal sucking a bitter lemon. Better risk he who merely looks bored silly. Soft soap with 'Have you lived here long?' or 'What do you do?' Not, under any circumstances, 'How long have you been playing bridge?', which might seem judgemental. Partner draws in his breath sharply and the world lurches into uncharted territory. Will the questionee respond? There is an awkward pause before the dam breaks and his face relaxes into a wonderful smile. Turns out he has a life history and a sense of humour. 'You got more out of him in five minutes than we have in five years,' says partner.

Avoid the opponent who looks as if he squirmed out of the birth canal sucking a bitter lemon.

Shame you now have to tackle new opponents, their egos riding high. They're always near the top of the rankings, a slick shark pairing. He fills out his plastic chair with gravitas, kilos and a crocodile smile, she chirrups away in her 'dim It girl from the 1920s' role. In the face of so much merriment, it's hard to concentrate. Don't they know it. Keep calm. This storm too will pass, often leaving serious wreckage on the results table. ...

DO ASK: *'Have you lived here long?, 'What do you do?'*
DON'T ASK: (under any circumstances) *'How long have you been playing bridge?'*

MAKING HAY

Now for those with whom you share the lower rungs of the ladder. This is where you could – and should – make hay. As in all competitions, neurosis creeps in as soon as you're faced with those you should beat. And they too have a well worked scheme. Left-hand opponent (LHO) taps his forefinger on his spread and mutters numbers under his breath. Honours, points, cards in each suit? As you try to identify a helpful pattern, right-hand opponent (RHO) snaps, 'Hold your cards up', as he cranes over to see them. He gives himself away by jumping the gun, interjecting before you can see your hand yourself. His words are designed to cover his intentions. Peeking is one thing, systematic cheating quite another.

DELAYED RESPONSE

On to super slow: 1C pass, 1D pass, the pause is beyond pregnant, no one speaks. When you have too few points to bid, you stare despairingly into space. How difficult can it be to work out what comes next? Thirty seconds pass, a minute. 1H from opener, hesitantly, cautiously. By now, responder needs a prompt: 'Your turn to bid.' She awakens from a reverie about Ivan, who takes her boot camp. So ripped, what a six pack, lovely pair of hands. ... Jerked unwillingly into the present, she stammers 1S. The opener is indecisive, time passes, he settles on 1NT.

The delayed response is the most aggravating form of gamesmanship. Yes, you should think before you bid, but there's only so much time to play each board. Cutting into it deliberately is taking advantage; so naturally it's commonplace. With the hand still to play, the ordeal is not over. You lead, briskly, fourth highest of longest suit as convention dictates. Cue pondering.... If you still have a board to play when the Director calls the next move, it's forfeited. If it's barely started, the other tables tap their fingers while you complete with indecent haste and unpredictable results. You could hate people for less.

FACE-OFF

The husband and wife combo come last. He has an opening bid, she responds, he supports, she hesitates on the rack of indecision. Four for game or leave it in three? Rosemary stares into a stony face which might have been carved out of Mount Rushmore in distant South Dakota. Her courage fails and she passes. He only makes three, so it's the right decision. 'I could tell from Robert's expression that he didn't want me to go on,' she giggles happily. Partner snarls, 'Director please.' He who rules walks over looking flustered. 'Unauthorised information,' says partner. 'She'd have raised to 4 and gone down but she said his face warned her not to.' The Director looks at the offending object, permanently set in a granite scowl; he shuffles his feet, seems embarrassed. 'Er ...', but we all know there is no retribution. A welcome diversion into bridge 'as theatre' is over.

MEA CULPA

But the possibility – certainty – of flouting the rules lies in wait for the unguarded rookie. As is customary with etiquette games (think golf, the sedentary *brigista*'s active sport of choice), there's a rule book, a deceptively slim yellow one published by the EBU that makes golf's Royal and Ancient bible seem oversimplified.

In routine contests, rulings are required more frequently on baize than on putting greens. You'll spot the Tournament Director (TD) on TV, answering golfer queries about legally replacing balls that end up under grandstands during the Open Championship, but he doesn't show up for your greensome at Heathland-on-Sea. However, the Director sits north at the top table at your bridge club, playing the session for free in return for services about to be rendered. Member's club-night table money may be as low as £2, so his saving is a miserable reward for a thankless task. If he's hassled, he won't be best pleased, especially if he's mid-play in a slam contract. Don't let that prevent you from disturbing him.

If you want to be sure of your rights, the bluffer should begin at the beginning (page 19) of the yellow book: 'Adjusted Score: a score awarded by the Director (see Law 12). It is either "artificial" or "assigned".'

Law 12, Director's Discretionary Powers (page 33) offers three full sides with three 'black type' subsections and eighteen subclauses. And read through to the end. Rule 93, Procedures of Appeal (page 117), again three major subsections, just the seven clauses.

The now enlightened bluffer has the firepower to stick his oar in. He can pay a refundable £40 to appeal to the English Bridge Union (EBU) against perceived misinterpretation of the rules, whether deliberately or through ignorance. Given Mafioso-style dominance in many clubs, justice may not be done and no love will be lost, but the bluffer has a voice – and he should use it, especially when bullying is involved. At some point, the room goes quiet as players settle to feed their obsession. A rogue mobile rings, heads swivel, venomous stares unleash, the culprit reddens, fumbles. 'Sorry. Thought

I'd turned it off. A new model. Sorry.' The room regains focus. 'Director please.' The shout rips the silence like a bullet. The Director rises wearily, gropes for the yellow book, approaches the table with a bright smile, as he's been taught at the Director's qualification course. 'How may I help you tonight?' Word perfect so far.

At this early stage, the most likely infringement is Lead out of Turn (LOOT). Before the rightful leader commits, he should put his card on the table face down and wait for his partner to say 'No questions' before he reveals it. That pause should prompt someone to say, 'It's not you to lead', but sometimes it doesn't. A relaxed declarer might allow opponents to correct, leaving the offending card face up on the table to be played as soon as legally possible. But most demand their kilos of flesh so the Director is called.

As it is impossible to pass the Director's course without memorising the five-choice spiel for LOOT, he's repeated it enough times in training to say it off pat. As he does, affably, patiently, trying to make it seem like sense. Four faces stare at him blankly, especially declarer's because it's he who must decide. Dare he accept the lead, putting his own hand down as dummy and letting partner play? Dangerously tempting, but grounds for divorce. So the Director must reiterate and reiterate some more until the dilemma is resolved. If you really want to go there, rules 54, 56 50D and 16C await ...

The other two common crimes against the Director's equilibrium are Insufficient Bid (IB) and revoke. The bluffer should appear to be familiar with both. Pulling out the wrong bidding card by mistake seems too trivial to disturb your own or anyone else's game. Wrong. LHO (left-hand opponent) responding ID to opener's IH can be construed as an attempt to give unauthorised information rather than a moment of distraction or reverie. It can be sanely and swiftly corrected by fast tracking the intended bid, but righteous indignation may not permit. In extremis, the Director may draw the IBer away from the table to grill him about intentions and comparable calls. A storm in a teacup? Or the Battle of Trafalgar?

REVOKING

Revoke, playing a different suit while you still have cards in the one led, is a pratfall. How stupid can you get? But you will. With lightning awareness, you can grab the offending card back without penalty, beyond laying it face up on the table for future use. More often you're unaware until you're outed, the revoke is established and you're condemned. The Director must assess tricks you may have gained or your opponents may have lost through your mistake. And award penalties accordingly. He won't like doing this so bluffers should know not to make a fuss. If, as can happen, opponents don't notice your revoke, it's not your duty to mention it. Silently give thanks for your lucky day.

If you're a repeat revoker, you could ask your club to adopt no-revoke decks, the club suit green, the diamond suit blue, the heart suit red, the spade suit black. This reduces the danger of pulling out the right colour in the wrong suit. A bluffer who suggests this sensible solution will be an object of derision. It's up to you.

GAMESMANSHIP?

Summoning the Director spills over into gamesmanship. Of course it does. It breaks the rhythm and unsettles opponents. It destroys his focus. The rule book offers infractions galore, many related to the will 'o the wisp intricacies of unauthorised information. This may be given accidentally, as in letting a card slip face up. Or intentionally, as in revealing stuff you'd like partner to know without getting caught. The wrong expression, the wrong inflexion, the wrong posture: all can be accountable in the wrong circumstances. Bluffers, of course, would never stoop to such behaviour.

A nerdy bluffer would impress by revealing that a Director scores around 4% less over the course of an average evening than he would without the burden of responsibility for his peers. As the Director is often one of the better players, his discomfiture should be your gain, but only if he's prevented from settling down to concentrate. A cunning operator uses the dark side of the rule book to make sure he can't. Calling him is also an antidote to boredom – a run of bad cards – or an antidote to bullying. There are no rules against shooting yourself in the foot.

ß

First referred to in 1529 in a published sermon by Bishop Latimer, bridge was also known as triumph, trump, slam, whisk, honors, ruff and swabbers; most of these terms are part of bridge today. Deploying trivia suggests levels of expertise you may never reach.

EVOLUTION AND ADAPTATION

As bridge's evolution is as opaque as its protocol, lobbing a cherished nugget into a chat can't easily be challenged. Whist, addictive among gentlemen with fortunes to lose on the turn of a card in London clubs from the mid-18th century, was the seedling. First referred to in 1529 in a published sermon by Bishop Latimer, it was also known as triumph, trump, slam, whisk, honors, ruff and swabbers; most of these terms are part of bridge today. Deploying trivia suggests levels of expertise you may never reach.

1854–56

When 14,000 British soldiers were stationed around Constantinople during the Crimean War, their officers trod the Galata Bridge across the Golden Horn to play cards in a coffeehouse. They called their game bridge – or so urban myth has it.

1874–90

Britch (Russian for whist) took root in the Khedival Club in Cairo where gamblers spiced it up as 'bridge whist', with doubles and redoubles but no auction. Those who avoided bankruptcy exported their expertise at *khedive* (as it was known) to the Riviera. So easy to fleece naive sunseekers on leave from British winters. Queen Victoria, a Nice regular in the Hotel Regina, may not have been amused but aristocrats living sumptuously on Nice's Promenade des Anglais and the Croisette in Cannes took up the challenge – and paid the price.

As bridge's evolution is as opaque as its protocol, lobbing a cherished nugget into a chat can't easily be challenged. Whist, addictive among gentlemen with mansions to lose on the turn of a card in London clubs from the mid-18th century, was the seedling.

Meanwhile, three bored Indian civil servants stranded on the outskirts of Empire in Uttar Pradesh were looking for a fourth. When their cries of 'anyone for whist' blew away in the hot desert wind, they played anyway; the fourth seat was designated as 'dummy', its cards played by the declarer as well as his own. The concept of giving a player a break was built into all subsequent versions.

Many welcome the chance to nip off to the bar for a sharpener when things are not going swimmingly.

1891

America's Kalamazoo Tray, the first duplicate board containing four pre-dealt hands ready for play, moved the goalposts towards public rather than private 'bridge whist'. Different pairs playing the same hands in rotation created a level playing field. Define level if you dare.

1893

Henry Barbey, French and Swiss on his mother's side, introduced the game he'd learned in Paris to the Whist Club in New York. His privately printed *Laws of Bridge* appeared a year earlier. He has a lot to answer for.

1892–94

Lord Brougham and Colonel Studdy, primed by military service in India and the Russo-Turkish War (1877–79), skirmished for bridge-whist priority toff rights at London's Portman and St George's Clubs.

1905

All the above melded and auction bridge was born. It said so in *The Times*. It was there to stay. Except it wasn't because it was far too simple.

1911–15

Until the declaration of the First World War, First Lord of the Admiralty Winston Churchill frequently played auction bridge aboard the luxurious Admiralty steam yacht, HMS *Enchantress*. During the day, he visited naval dockyards and launched battleships in Britain and the Mediterranean. In the evenings, he often played his newly adopted card game with such exalted guests as Prime Minister Asquith, his daughter Violet and Second Sea Lord, Prince Louis of Battenberg.

1918–25
As is customary, the French were perfecting being different. They called their game *plafond* (ceiling) and included the first contract element: players had to predict how many tricks they'd make during bidding. A key breakthrough, but the Americans couldn't leave it at that.

1925
Eureka! Harold Stirling Vanderbilt, fourth generation railroad multi-millionaire, found himself with time to spare while cruising on the *Finland* from Los Angeles to Havana. He used it to assemble contract bridge from the component parts of auction and *plafond*. He added vulnerability, bonuses for slams, points for making a contract and penalties for failure. He accommodated dummy. By his scoring system, the best of three games wins the rubber (like sets in tennis). Back in New York, Henry distributed a few copies of his master plan to auction Bridgemates. Too rich to be modest, he said, 'I made no other efforts to publicise it. Thanks apparently to its excellence, it popularised itself and spread like wildfire.'

Bluffers will earn top brownie points for a mention of the first day Vanderbilt and his mates played contract bridge: 1 November 1925, as the *Finland* left the dock in Balboa to pass through the Panama Canal.

The Culbertson Golden Age

Ely Culbertson, born to an American mining engineer and a Russian mother in Romania in 1891, far outpointed Vanderbilt as a self-promotional big beast. He learned six modern languages plus Latin and classical Greek at the Sorbonne and the University of Geneva, then taught himself the rudiments of several more. After the Russian Revolution, the young opportunist deployed his linguistic skills at high stakes bridge and poker tables in European cities. Presumably he also had a head for figures.

When he ran out of willing victims, Culbertson moved across the Atlantic to conquer the New World. Two years later, he married auction bridge teacher, Josephine Murphy Dillon, in New York. Together they produced four children and set out to rule the world of bridge.

DON'T SAY: (As you throw a cup of coffee at your partner) *'Nothing serious. There was no sugar in it'*.
DO SAY*: When you acquire a good partner, better mollify rather than moan or maul.'*

1929

The first issue of *Bridge World*, publisher E. Culbertson, asked for an international Code of Laws. America, France and Britain supplied one for publication in November, 1932. Rules and more rules – the thin edge of the wedge got thicker.

1930

With Henry Vanderbilt on America's Cup duty – he won in 1930 and 1937 – Ely Culbertson grabbed centre stage. Propelled by his gluttony for showmanship, his *Contract Bridge Blue Book* was an instant bible. The first salvo in the Great Systems Wars had been fired.

1930

Blue Book vs British Bridge: Lieutenant Colonel Walter Buller challenged the great American to a 200-rubber match in London. After puncturing the colonel's considerable ego, Culbertson dealt equally easily with the team from Crockfords (legendary Mayfair gaming club named for William Crockford who founded it in 1828) captained by another military officer, Colonel Henry 'Pops' Beasley, a leading British contract bridge player of the day.

1931

The Bridge Battle of the Century. Culbertson's challenger was Chicago-born Sidney Lenz, intent on proving that his Official System as presented in Bridge Headquarters was the superior format. Disembarking from the *Mauritania* on his return from London, Ely was dismissive: 'His system is 80% Culbertson, 12% work and Lenz, 8% rubbish.' As the outraged Lenz took the train to New York, he was intent on retribution.

December 1931–January 1932

Game on: playing with up and coming great Oswald Jacoby, Lenz led through 43 rubbers, but the partnership crashed and burned as Lenz dared to criticise his partner's aggressive play. By the time Jacoby quit on rubber 103, Culbertson, who completed 88 rounds with Josephine (generally considered to be the better player), was well ahead. Lenz regained ground with his second partner but his adversary was out of reach. Note to self: when you acquire a good partner, better mollify rather than moan or maul.

With animosity as its trigger and Culbertson's showmanship at its heart, the series put bridge in a spotlight that has never shone on it again. Radio supplied hand by hand commentary and newspapers printed front page bulletins in 30 countries.

1932–36
Culbertson is king, his team unbeaten in international challenges and tournaments. He and his entourage swept around the world in a blaze of glory, but London remained his happiest hunting ground. Regular victim, Henry Ingram, pointed out that the Brits had day jobs while the American visitors didn't get up till lunch time. Amateur vs pro. So little changes. ...

1937
Team Culbertson finally lost to Austria's tyrannical Paul Stern in the International Bridge League (IBL) World Championship in Budapest. With three victories out of five since the inaugural tournament in the Netherlands in 1932, the volatile Austrian captain basked in European admiration for his flair, though not for his behaviour. On one occasion, he threw a cup of coffee at his partner. 'Nothing serious,' he commented. 'There was no sugar in it.' (Note to bluffers: just don't do it.)

1938

The Culbertsons divorced and Ely quit tournament bridge. Josephine kept the surname – as you would – and continued her chosen career. Her ex campaigned for world peace. Even as Chamberlain travelled to Munich to appease Hitler, he sensed it was a less stressful option than bridge.

1950

The Bermuda Bowl was inaugurated in the mid-Atlantic archipelago in 1950 by resident accountant Norman Bach. The first Bowl, contested by North America, Europe and Britain, went across the Atlantic. Likewise the second, a straight fight between the American Contract Bridge League and the European Bridge League (represented by Italy) in Naples. And the third, against Sweden in New York. The first multinational European team, competing in Monaco in 1955, was also defeated.

1955

Great Britain re-emerged, qualifying to take on North America in New York by beating 13 Euro nations in Montreux. They won handsomely. Time for bluffers to drop the essential bridge names Terence Reese and Boris Schapiro into the mix. Read on. ...

1958

The Bermuda Bowl, unofficially recognised as the World Championships, permanently included the best of South America – in this instance Argentina.

A VERY BRITISH SCANDAL

Cut to Buenos Aires in **1965** where teams from Italy, North America, Great Britain and the host nation gathered to contest the Bermuda Bowl. Leading for GB, Terence Reese and Boris Schapiro, acknowledged world champions, but perhaps too brilliant and surely too arrogant for their own good. 'Bridge reveals character. A man who in ordinary life gets by as a sound and well adjusted citizen may show himself at the bridge table to be stupid, vain, obstinate, greedy and dishonest.' Time would reveal that Reese would have been wiser to keep such thoughts to himself.

ARCHETYPAL GENTLEMAN

As every bridge bluffer should be ready to recount, Reese was an archetypal privileged Englishman of his time, born in Epsom, Surrey in 1913, educated at boarding school (Bradfield), a classics scholar at New College, Oxford: he graduated in 1935 with a double first. His parents, a banker turned caterer and a mother who ran a hotel near Guildford in conjunction with a bridge club, famously met as First Gentleman and First Lady at a whist drive. Their son played beggar-my-neighbour avidly before he could read and auction bridge (contract had not yet been invented) from aged seven, hiding behind a cushion to sort his cards.

'Bridge reveals character. A man who in ordinary life gets by as a sound and well adjusted citizen may show himself at the bridge table to be stupid, vain, obstinate, greedy and dishonest.'

Disgraced former world champion Terence Reese

He captained the bridge team at Oxford, winning the inaugural Varsities match in 1935, against a Cambridge team led by the future Chancellor of the Exchequer, Ian Macleod. A year at Harrods put him off commerce. Instead he joined the staff of *British Bridge World* and co-wrote his first book in 1937. He avoided direct action in the Second World War by signing up for Air Raid Precautions (ARP) and taking a job in a factory making blackout curtains owned by fellow bridge player, Pedro Juan. He was seen there on occasion, notably when forewarned that the Ministry of Labour was looking for him. At other times, he was at Crockfords. Cue loud explosion. Agitated member, 'My God, they've got the War Office.' Reese, selecting another card from dummy, 'Not intentionally, surely.'

When hostilities ended, he became a world-class international, a prolific columnist in newspapers and magazines, an author of some 90 bridge books, a witty radio personality. And then in 1944, he met the man who would become his nemesis. ...

THE ARRIVISTE

Where Reese indulged in mandarin detachment with a cutting edge, Schapiro was boisterous, loud-mouthed, offensively rude, aggressively crude. A dedicated lothario, he'd say 'Fancy a bit of adultery?' to women straying into his orbit. A jolly jest (even a compliment) in the 1940s, actionable today.

He was born in Latvia in 1909 into a wealthy bloodstock family. At the time of the Russian Revolution, the Schapiros relocated to Yorkshire, continuing to supply horses for carriages and buses in Europe and beyond, a business that led to friendships with Saudi royals. By the time he was ten, Boris was playing cards for money but his teenage trophies were for show jumping rather than bridge. As horses were replaced by combustion engines, the Schapiros switched to the meat trade. (A worrying development – don't go there.)

CHALK AND CHEESE

At the table, as everywhere else, Reese and Schapiro were chalk and cheese. Terence was the Roundhead, clinical, accurate, devastating. Boris was the Cavalier, excitable, irascible, intuitive. In championship terms, the chemistry worked and prestigious trophies accrued. But that didn't make them the best of friends. Reese's sense of humour revelled in japes he contrived himself, but he was never a happy butt of other people's jokes.

The cynical bluffer might recall the time he left the Schapiro flat in Belgravia's Eaton Square carrying a pillow case filled with his share of the silverware. On the street, he was stopped by a policeman. No problem, Boris would vouch for him. When he opened his door, Schapiro was quick to spot an opportunity. 'Never seen this man in my life, officer.' By the time he was released after hours in custody, Reese was seriously unamused.

On another occasion, Shapiro bet £50 – big bucks back then – that he could replace himself as dummy with a naked woman without distracting Reese from play. As he did. 'Notice anything unusual about that one?' Boris enquired. 'Yes, a delicate situation in hearts,' Terence replied. Small wonder he didn't get married until he was 57.

THE LITTLE MAJOR

Was the edginess between them the subconscious genesis of the great Buenos Aires hearts scandal? The unassuming trigger had become known as the *Little Major*. In the belief that a rash of conventions was ruining the game, Reese cooked up a facetious variant to end the false bidding fever. His system promoted every one-level bid as artificial. No one could take that seriously. Ironically he tried it, fell in love with it and promoted it, both as a recognised bidding system and with reluctant partners, among them Boris Schapiro.

By the time the two men reached Buenos Aires, Schapiro refused to play it. Even so, Reese persuaded Schapiro to share a finger signalling routine involving hearts in the opening game against the North Americans. Unthinkable maybe, but some still take it into account in guilty–innocent disputes that rage on over half a century later.

V-FORMATION

Add a bluffer's bonus for naming the American whistleblower, B. Jay Becker. 'Dorothy Hayden and I were playing against Reese and Schapiro on the first day of our match against Great Britain, and we were about one-third through the evening session's play when I happened to look over at Reese on my right and noticed that he was holding his cards with two fingers spread in V-style in front of his cards. It meant very little to me at the time, but it struck me subconsciously that this was an uncomfortable way to hold cards.' Try it and you'll see he's right.

'I will never know whether this fleeting observation would have made a lasting impression on me except that when I looked at Schapiro on my left on the very same deal I observed that he was holding his cards with the same two fingers (index and middle) in a V formation.'

After the game, Becker approached Mrs Hayden. 'Dorothy, I'm sorry to have to tell you this, but I think we were cheated tonight.' To her credit, the lady didn't faint or yell, calmly allowing Becker to explain his thinking and gradually warming to his interpretation.

'Went into the pit against Reese and Schapiro. Something terrible is going on. I could not believe my eyes.'

Dorothy Hayden, four times world bridge champion

The couple had to wait for three days to take on Reese/Schapiro again. From Hayden's diary: 'Went into the pit against Reese and Schapiro. B [Becker] is right. Something terrible is going on. I could not believe my eyes. I watched every hand. The movements are very natural and graceful. The fingers do not register unless you know what to look for. How can they do this in front of a whole grandstand of people. '

OUT OF THE BAG

The cat was out of the bag. Becker told John Gerber, the American non-playing captain, and Brixton-born player-journalist, Alan Truscott, who was covering the tournament for the *New York Times*. They, along with Great Britain captain, Ralph Swimer, watched Reese and Schapiro digging the pit deeper against other teams. As a former maths teacher and actuary, Hayden analysed the finger movements and came up with the correct solution – the varying spreads indicated how many hearts each player held (from 0–7).

After an investigation, the World Bridge Federation (WBF), monitoring the Buenos Aires tournament, confirmed 'certain irregularities' and banned the pair from international competition by a 10–0 vote. Their matches were forfeited and they went home in disgrace, while Truscott, by now more American than the Americans, made sure the scandal filled front pages around the world.

In London, the Beatles were accepting MBEs and David Bailey was marrying Catherine Deneuve with Mick Jagger as his best man. In a mini-skirted world rocking to Brit hits, bridge was a bastion of old values. The scandal threatened the country's cherished self-image for sportsmanship in adverse circumstances. *'Let us be glad, but not because of winning, Let us go home one family today'*, as the 1948 London Olympic hymn put it.

In a break with protocol, the WBF left the sentencing to the home nation. The British Bridge League pounced with a tribunal top-loaded with useful witnesses for the defence. Conveniently, an eminent but bridge-ignorant QC was the appointed judge. After 60 sessions over 19 months, he declared Reese and Schapiro not guilty: 'The circumstantial evidence gives rise to doubt. However, there is no indication of cheating evident in the action or the play,' he declared.

At some stage bluffers will be invited to step up to the witness box and offer their own judgment: innocent or guilty? This is a tricky one because both Reese and Schapiro actually confessed to finger signalling, but as research for a book Reese was planning. Both went to their graves protesting their innocence. Schapiro got in before he left Argentina during a walk with Swimer in a Buenos Aires park. Did he really say, 'That wicked man made me do it'? Swimer would swear under oath that he had, adding 'I saw them [Reese and Schapiro] cheating with my own eyes.' Schapiro would later deny the remark.

Reese responded. 'Hardly fair comment by Boris, wickedness didn't come into it.' As world champions it would be unthinkable they'd cheat so no one would notice, he'd assured the reluctant Schapiro. In any case, they wouldn't use the information to benefit during play. Card analysis seems to confirm they didn't. The price of Boris's cooperation was transparency: the signalling would eventually be revealed in full in Reese's book, along with evidence that they hadn't used illegally gained intel to improve their results.

And the other assurance was that it should be published soon. It wasn't. Reese's DNA was never wired for failure. Part of his agenda was to show how easy it was to use simplistic signalling to get away with cheating. When he discovered it wasn't, he summarily abandoned his project and his partner without a moment's remorse.

AFTERMATH

That his arrogance made him so sure he'd never be detected is a given, but the risk of trading universal acclaim for global derision would surely need a further spur. Disenchantment, boredom, the inevitability of future decline? Whichever, he quit at the top of his game and died an indifferent backgammon obsessive from aspirin poisoning in 1982. Verdict? Accidental death.

Schapiro rode out his ban and returned to

competition as a geriatric ogre. In 1999, he won the World Senior Pairs (for over 55s) at a record aged 89. At his landmark birthday party a year later, guests included fellow addicts, Omar Sharif and Prince Khalid Abdullah of Saudi Arabia. During his 91st year, Boris added further joy to his celebrations by verbally abusing his partner during the European Senior Teams. Shocked opponents called the referee to protect the victim. The official ruled in favour of Schapiro by granting him a special dispensation for the over 90s. Old men behaving badly? Bluffers should never underestimate them.

As no one can see their partner, surely it's got to be foolproof? Maybe for the common herd, but these guys haven't reached the upper echelons without guile and nerve.

CROSSING THE ETHICAL LINE

The overtly respectable world of professional bridge is still occasionally rocked by claims that top players have been involved in cheating but, after Buenos Aires, the authorities hatched schemes to make it harder. In today's national and international competitions, a screen divides the table diagonally, north and east on one side, south and west on the other. After a foot tapping scandal in 1975, screens were extended down to the floor. Bidding behind the screen means putting each duplicate board in the centre of a frame with four felt side trays. This is pushed under the screen in rotation so that each player can consider the bids, then place his own bidding card in the appropriate tray. As no one can see their partner, surely it's got to be foolproof? Maybe for the common herd, but these guys haven't reached the upper echelons without guile and nerve.

Like most systems, this one has an Achilles heel,

in the shape of a little flap in the centre of the screen. Once the auction is done, the lead is placed face down on the table and dummy reveals his hand as the flap flips up. Players can see each other's hands (physically rather than the cards), but not their bodies. No scope for fingered hearts or diamond brooches. Time for more astute shenanigans.

Golf is the blueprint for systematic cheating, not only because it took root before bridge, but because expansive Elysian fields are perfect for picking up and shifting, improving and wrongly identifying a small ball. In the days when caddies were de rigueur, a ten bob note passed discreetly to your loyal bag carrier guaranteed that the right things happened – rolling an identical ball down a trouser leg in the approximate place the first was lost has always been popular and rewardable. In one well-documented case before cameras ruled, the ruse allegedly won an Open Championship. Was the caddie paid off for life, aka blackmail? Winning majors can create great wealth, but we'll never know.

With high-level competition dominated by referees hovering menacingly over play-by-play footage, deception in both golf and bridge is much harder to hide. In today's caddie-free zones, a golfer has to do the dirty deed himself. A cautionary tale from Elie golf course in Scotland where a vintage submarine periscope at the starter's hut protects player safety on holes on the backside of the first hill. Starter, sardonically: 'You got out of the bunker at the fourth remarkably well, Miss Jones.'

On a bridge table's limited playing field, cheating requires greater ingenuity. Of course the bluffer displays exemplary detachment from systematic infringement, but he's aware that legal signalling is encouraged and explained in every annual ever written. For the elite, it's an essential tool to say which suits they'd like led and which not, how many cards they have in each suit – odd or even numbers – and where the honours lie. For the pack, it's a maze of indecision. The rewards are great, the scope for tragic misunderstanding far greater. Chico Marx knew how to dodge that bullet. 'If you like my lead', he told Harpo, 'don't bother to signal with a high card. Just smile and nod your head.'

In the olden days, chain smoking at the tables provided invaluable signals. Lighters, fags, fingers and smoke were deployed with precision and artistry in the service of illegal communication.

SOFT CHEATING

This happens in the grey area between the letter and the spirit of the law. Tempo is an integral issue. If east over-pauses for reflection before saying, 'No bid', north or south can deny west his bid if they think he might be benefitting from unauthorised information – a prolonged pause may suggest east has nearly enough points to open or respond; zilch would invite a swifter response, even when unaccompanied by an angry shrug.

If this causes indignation, as it very well may, players call the Director for a verdict.

Whether or not east's extended reflection is innocent, it's hard to prove, though not so hard as deliberately devious methods of seducing opponents into making rubbish decisions. The so-called Alcatraz Coup prompts an opponent to react – a 'tell' – in the hope of determining the location of a vital card. In the Sominex Coup, declarer pauses lengthily to bore others into errors – possibly related to somnolent, as in a drug for sending them to sleep. The bluffer who scatters nuggets about coups that cross moral lines can expect blank stares – or hostile speculation about his own ethics.

In the olden days, chain smoking at the tables provided invaluable signals. Lighters, fags, fingers and smoke were deployed with precision and artistry in the service of illegal communication. These days the ubiquity of smoking bans has largely closed off this little avenue of pleasure.

HARD CHEATING

... is pre-planned and very difficult to detect when executed seamlessly, as the following examples illustrate.

Fulvio Fantoni and Claudio Nunes: Italian professionals ranked one and two in the world when they played for Monaco in the 2014 European Bridge Championships. *Method*: when either led, he placed the card vertically if he had future control – honours or a void in that suit – and horizontally if he didn't. Both denied the accusation but, after three separate investigations, the Italian Bridge Federation banned them for three years in March 2016.

The Coughing Doctors: Distinguished German medics Michael Elinescu and Entscho Wladow used coded coughs to win the World Bridge Championships in Bali in 2013. Maybe they got the idea from Charles Ingram, the coughing major who won £1 million on TV's *Who Wants to Be a Millionaire* in 2003. Like him, they lost the loot. Stripped of their gold medals, they were banned from WBF tournaments for life and from individual competition for ten years.

Lotan Fisher and Ron Schwartz: New generation superstars from the day they won the World Junior Teams Championships in 2010. Despite proof of cheating in childhood, the brash and outspoken Fisher was hailed as the 'wonder boy of Israeli bridge'. In the European Youth Bridge Championship in 2011, he partnered the understated Schwartz in the winning team. Invitations to major events followed. Unlike chess, bridge is not a prodigy game: experience counts, so most juveniles have to put in the hard hours before they get big wins. Fisher and Schwartz rolled up and took the world by storm with uncanny intuitive brilliance. The mandarins watched and clapped: youth is highly prized, because it takes the game forward.

Method: positioning the board containing the cards.

When the auction ends and before the flap goes up, the duplicate board is removed from the cumbersome bidding tray and placed in the correct orientation on the table. Usually this is done by north and south, the positions Fisher and Schwartz always tried to secure. The system: board pushed forward under the screen, please lead a spade; with one corner peeping under the screen, a heart; half and half, a diamond; none of the board projecting under the screen, a club; totally unseen until the flap rises, no preference. Leads are one of the hardest things to get right: with preferential insights, trophies are much much easier to win. As are the super rich sponsors who pay pros to join their teams. The better the results, the larger the payday.

'I always felt there was cheating in bridge. I just didn't realise the extent, or the level that the players who were caught cheating were at.'
Zia Mahmood, World Grand Master

The Whistleblower

In 2014 and 2015, Team Schwartz (above), captained by American Richie Schwartz (no relation), had a string of stellar triumphs. One of the young Israelis' teammates, Boye Brogeland, a small-town Norwegian professional in his 40s, had heard rumours that his young *co-equipiers* were making successful plays requiring improbably

Sherlockian powers of deduction. He warned Fisher about the tittle tattle and urged him to keep it clean.

The following year, the young Israelis were courted by Jimmy Cayne, the bridge-playing CEO of global investment bank Bear Sterns in a sponsorship deal that prompted Brogeland (who had been rejected) to go public. He and his three non-Israeli teammates, Boye announced primly, would give up everything they'd won together, as all players should if their team had contained a 'cheating pair'. 'Boye had balls as big as church bells to do what he was doing,' said American bridge champion Jeff Meckstroth admiringly. He then backed up the Scandinavian's growing 'clean bridge' campaign by helping to out Fantoni and Nunes. As all bridge cheats do, Fisher and Schwartz protested their innocence in the face of suspension by the Israeli Bridge Federation. They were banned from playing in European bridge competitions for five years, and banned from playing as a partnership for life.

'I always felt there was cheating in bridge,' said the legendary Pakistani-born superstar, Zia Mahmood, an inductee into the American Contract Bridge Hall of Fame in 2007. 'I just didn't realise the extent, or the level that the players who were caught cheating were at.'

_B_

*At dinner, where the organisers'
'placements' should encourage new
friendships, they rearrange the names so
they can discuss Aurelio and Artemis's
prowess in short tennis and lacrosse,
saxophone, vegan rugby and violin.*

BRIDGE STAYCATION

By convention, bridge holidays offer expert tuition and duplicate play, so read the small print before deciding what's best. Some schedules are laughably lightweight, some intriguingly pitched, some dangerously intense. The bluffer is encouraged to endure agonising intro drinks and meals as appropriate to the holiday's cost. Even if you don't like the seating arrangement when it's time to eat, a good book is not a viable dinner plan.

THE SOCIAL UPLANDS

For the solo bluffer, bridge holidays are high risk. Danger number one is the clique. You've left your bridge comfort zone for pastures new – bravely, foolishly? The plan is to share an elegant weekend in a Cotswolds hideaway with like-minded strangers. No partner required. Or so the bumph assured you. In the foyer, however, the sound of braying. Not, unfortunately, agricultural beasts of burden, but a quartet of blondes abusing received pronunciation raucously. Within seconds, everyone is aware that Camilla,

Cordelia, Clara and Carmela are taking a break from rich men and spoiled kids. That they're joined together at the honed hip by years at Marlborough, Cheltenham Ladies, or Roedean. That they're not on this planet to mingle with peasants. Intentionally or unintentionally, they drive a forklift truck through a mini break. From the outset, they're in country house overdrive. At drinks and canapés – their beloved cocktail party showcase – they exchange anecdotes of mummies and daddies playing cards in drawing rooms owned by the Cunningham-Bullers. At dinner, where the organisers' *placement* should encourage new friendships, they rearrange the names so they can discuss Aurelio and Artemis's prowess in short tennis and lacrosse, saxophone, vegan rugby and violin. Co-diners fail to hide their mounting desperation. In the card room, they ask idiot questions at tuition sessions, neighing and whinnying to establish priority as teacher's pet. If people book as a four, the organisers won't ask them to split up but elitism makes others feel excluded. Rudeness might dent their certainty that social status makes them bullet proof, but that's inappropriate in a Georgian rectory turned boutique hotel. Bluffers must wait for the right moment to casually drop an entirely imaginary game with Bill Gates into the conversation. Did you win, they ask uncertainly. A wry and modest smile: 'I take a Corinthian view. For me it's not about the winning.'

OFF-PEAK CHEAPIE

Brigistas are known for short arms and long pockets so budget conscious obsessives should think about a seaside town in winter – somewhere like Worthing comes to mind. Tall houses in dishevelled Victorian squares have long been converted into rabbit warren hotels, crammed at the height of the Sussex Riviera summer, empty in the shoulder seasons, desolate though overheated in January. This is a perennially happy hunting ground for 'Mr Bridge', aka Bernard McGee, and his many fans. With so many empty rooms, there is no singles supplement. Bluffers love that sort of economy.

If the bluffer can't win here, he can't win anywhere. As a place to polish his bluffing technique it is hard to improve on, because nobody really cares if he's rubbish. Everyone is a newbie at some stage.

THE FANATIC'S OPTION

If you're hungry for progress, accelerate your opportunities at an EBU Congress. This is an aspirational name for a bridge-saturated break. They crop up all over, including foreign parts. The grander the name the more rarefied the aspirations.

Again, you can't go alone but with EBU rankings at stake up for grabs, you need to be aware of the obstacles. Every *duplicateer* has an EBU rating which rises – or falls – every time he plays at an affiliated club. Improving it is a conundrum: if the bluffer plays with a duffer, he'll sink out of sight; if he plays with a star, he may rise. Or the star's brilliance may be humiliatingly dimmed, causing his own hard-won handicap to regress. He won't like that, so the bluffer must find – persuade? – someone to take the risk.

ALTERNATIVE ACTION

As a rule of thumb, the smarter the hotel and the better the food, the more incidental the bridge. If guests can be persuaded to enjoy spa, massage, indoor pool and pleasure gardens, the organisers have quality time to read a book. So much more rewarding than explaining the Unassuming Cue Bid or the Unusual 2NT all over again. In the morning the resident expert can't dodge the tuition bullet, in the evening there shall be duplicate, gentle or savage, but better all round that punters should take a healthy walk after lunch.

BRIDGE-GOLF

From the organiser's point of view, bridge and golf is the perfect combo. Those who play bridge often play golf and vice versa. If you need proof, spot the number of golfers dealing cards over a cup of tea and crustless egg and cress sandwiches in golf club bars nationwide. Both games take hours and their rule books are maddeningly verbose. Both games are handicap-driven: everyone is elated by rise, devastated by plummet.

So much for the mechanics. In the mind, the differences are more rewardingly pronounced. As a rough guide, the fewer intimations of disaster, the better the golfer; the more intuitive the bidding, the more cunning the play, the better the *brigista*. Meanwhile, the following acronyms might assist the bluffer to get there sooner rather than later. Or at least understand why progress is not as rapid as might have been hoped.

Golf: VSSF

Visualise: the shot you'd like to make, in the almost certain knowledge you won't be able to.

Set-up: the unnatural angles that are allegedly perfect for launching golf balls many yards in the direction of a tin cup sunk into a hole 4.25 inches in diameter.

Swing: grooved by hours of practice, yet as mysteriously unpredictable as a sack of snakes. No heavy lifting of head, body, left arm, right hip. ...

Focus: exorcise the demons implicit in V, S & S and you'll be a winner.

Bridge: ABPI

Assess: the value of the hand, noting oddities, potential traps.

Bid: according to the selected system, with leeway for intuition.

Plan: the play, with scope for changes of direction as things develop.

Imagine: even when you've taken all this into account, think outside the box.

Working out the best route through the minefield is the secret of success. This may suggest there's no natural correlation between excellence at bridge and golf. Perfect say the organisers, we'll keep all of the people happy some of the time. And our afternoons are free. For all concerned, the best scenario is a hotel with a golf course: no need to organise transport or answer directions queries.

Take as an example a bridge-golf holiday hotel on Norfolk's north-eastern curve. The Links Country Park

Hotel is an imposing Edwardian pile with an indoor pool and a golf course opened in 1903. 'One of the best 9 holes you'll ever play', is hardly an original claim. Nor necessarily false in this case, but for discerning golfers, the cherry on the cake is a period billet between the Sheringham and Royal Cromer cliff top clubs.

Steam trains sometimes chug along the North Norfolk Railway, much as they did when Sheringham opened in 1891. A chance then for bluffers to name drop the celebrated golf writer Bernard Darwin. 'At Sheringham', the distinguished future *Times* correspondent wrote in 1910, 'we shall be called upon to do only a moderate amount of climbing but some of the stoutest hitting with the brassey that there has ever been required of us.' The Cromer course dates back to 1888 and was regalised by the future King Edward VII, a friend and playing partner of the first president, Lord Suffield. Infamously susceptible to coastal erosion, Darwin records seeing the 17th hole topple peacefully into the 'German Ocean'.* Several celebrated golf architects have since held erosion at bay and Cromer still has 18 rewardingly varied holes. For the bluffer, battling hostile forces – gales, gorse, gremlins – on historic links is a plausible excuse for playing bad bridge later. Deploy with caution – you won't be the only one to use it.

DO SAY: *'Sorry, golf was a nightmare this afternoon. Must explain my lousy bridge this evening.'.*

---

* Also known as the 'North Sea'. Darwin does not record whether anyone was on the 17th tee at the time.

DON'T SAY: *'The holes at Cromer have been falling into the sea for a century or more so playing there triggers risk addiction – leading to overbidding at evening bridge.'*

BRIDGE-CROQUET

If bridge combo holiday seekers are golf refuseniks, croquet is an increasingly popular alternative. And arguably one better suited to bridge players. As in golf, the head must stay down, but the basic swing is easily learned. Stalk the ball to find the correct line, take the mallet back and bring it through smoothly, with or without follow through, depending on the shot you want to make. What could possibly go wrong? Association croquet (AC) is a very wily contest, worthy of bridge or chess brains in terms of strategy and tactics. The bridge-croquet hosted combo holiday is in its infancy, but bluffers should know that Guyers House Hotel in Pickwick outside Bath is a promising pioneer. Built as a farmhouse in 1670, its mellow Bath stone walls expanded in Quaker ownership over the centuries. Today's gracious architectural hybrid stands in six acres of gardens. More than enough for a full-size croquet lawn (and a tennis court). And 37 bedrooms is ideal for a surprisingly competitive bridge break, sometimes unexpectedly mellow compared to blood letting among the hoops.

CAFE-BRIDGE

This increasingly popular day out in a town with cafes and restaurants seeking gain on slow mornings has seen bridge clubs outreaching into the community. The most civilised version of the concept is a decent restaurant with a side room to set up for play. The tables are tiny, the crush increased by the need to keep wall mirrors out of sight lines. The duplicate session starts after coffee and finishes in time for lunch, your choices pre-ordered a couple of weeks before. The food is delicious, the all-in price advantageous, the conviviality contagious. The alternative format is rolling play, with walks between cafes until it's time for lunch. Best if it's not raining.

BRIDGEATHON

Not to be confused with the London Bridgeathon, an event in aid of Haematology Cancer Care which involves crossing all bridges on a six-mile stretch of the Thames. In the interests of food and beverage, clubs sometimes use the term for a hyper weekend with sessions morning, noon and night. Enjoyable, but arranging your own is even more fun. Recruit three fellow travellers for afternoon duplicate at an all-day club like Andrew Robson, repair to a bar for play afterwards, book into a friendly restaurant for cards over and after dinner. That's the full nine hours, less only the time it takes to walk between venues.

COMPUTER-BRIDGE

Available for free or a fee: download the relevant app and get stuck in. Be aware it can be very addictive and may seriously damage your eyesight. Bridge Base Online, partly owned by Bill Gates, is the market leader. The French-owned Funbridge is a compelling alternative. They and their rivals have practice exercises, daily 20-board ratings tournaments and monthly ratings tournaments, with upgrading to the next level if you reach the required percentage. For a fee, contestants can enter tournaments offering master points to improve their handicaps or IMPs to improve their regional rankings. These can be played anonymously or, for the seriously courageous, with real strangers who may not hold back on cyber insults. Or you can take on strangers with your real life partner.

The value of remote bridge is debatable – and hotly debated. 'Peter's always at it, but it hasn't done him any good', a *duplicateer* might snigger. Others love it, albeit defensively in the face of such derision. Some national players find it useful as a practice tool. Others may use it but not admit it. As with books, the moral high ground is with the paper version, but the e-reader has its uses too.

ß

Historically the French government took playing cards very seriously. Regulations imposed between 1780 and 1945, required watermarked paper (proof state tax had been paid) and 'portraits officiels' (official portraits), historical or mythical, on all court cards.

HAVE CARDS, WILL TRAVEL

The bluffer might consider doing some cursory research into playing bridge overseas, and how the game has evolved differently across the world. It will help to cement the impression that he has travelled widely in pursuit of 'developing' his game.

ON THE CARDS

Playing cards, as the bluffer will already know, were invented in China during the Tang dynasty (9th-century AD). They doubled as gaming tools and currency, a cunning way of circumventing betting regulations. With cash on the line, the suits were coin multiples: simple coins, strings of coins, myriads of strings of coins, tens of myriads (20,000) of strings of coins. *Pre-brigistas* played *madiao,* the first known trick-taking game, during the Ming Dynasty (1368–1644).

Four-suited playing cards – cups, coins, swords and polo sticks – appeared in the Mamluk Sultanate (now Cairo) in Egypt circa 1370, and in France by 1377.

Today's French pack evolved from the Latin system (also used in Italy, Spain and Portugal). *Trefles, carreaux, coeur, piques, sans atout* (clover, tiles, hearts, pikes, no trumps) covers the playing sequence, with *valet, dame, roi and as* making up the honours. Early versions had Egyptian honours: king, viceroy, deputy. The French endorsed female emancipation by replacing the viceroy with the queen in the 15th century, adding the ace as top honour when kings went out of fashion after the Revolution.

Historically the French government took playing cards very seriously. Regulations imposed between 1780 and 1945, required watermarked paper (proof state tax had been paid) and *portraits officiels* (official portraits), historical or mythical, on all court cards. King of diamonds Julius Caesar, king of clubs Alexander the Great, queen of spades Pallas Athena, queen of hearts Judith (she of the head of Holofernes), jack of diamonds Hector, jack of clubs Lancelot. Pack numbers varied from 32 to 52. Suits too: a German province added a fifth, but it never really caught on. Thank heavens: a five-sided bridge table would be hard to handle.

The Germanic deck competed vigorously with the Latin one from the late 1370s onwards. With a less confrontational line-up of acorns, leaves, hearts and bells, it dominated the Saxon and Prussian heartlands, Switzerland and the Austro-Hungarian Empire. Spain and Italy prefer swords, cups, clubs and coins, the variant they spread to Latin and South America. The Americans introduced the joker, a key component in a game called 'euchre', in the 18th century. And eventually they all turned to bridge. Bluffers rejoice: who could dispute any of that?

BRIDGE MECCAS

So now you know what to expect when you ask the concierge to set up a game in a five-star 'Palace' in Portugal or Switzerland or France. If he's any use, he'll call in local residents. They're already familiar with the bridge room, where the mirrors reflect most efficiently, where the setting sun gets in opponents' eyes, where the afternoon tea should be set up – probably at your expense. Take your pick of any of the following bridge meccas, and claim to be a regular:

Reid's Palace, Madeira: excellent base for sampling the eponymous drink, playing golf at Paleiro and imitating Lady Prudence Jellicoe, defying her Christian name in a dramatic swallow dive off the hotel's high-diving board circa 1930. That's about when bridge hit the card room. The afternoon tea is iconic. **Cards:** swords, cups, clubs and coins.

Badrutt's Palace, St Moritz: popular with Euro royals and Hollywood stars. Famous for ice polo, cricket, horse racing on the lake below, and the notorious Cresta Run – guaranteed to unsettle the bowels of the most experienced tobogganist. Live harpist for breakfast. **Cards:** acorns, leaves, hearts and bells.

Le Negresco, Nice: roughly the same age as auction bridge, well located on the Promenade des Anglais close to the Old Town. Gold Key concierges are there to help: 'they love challenges so don't hesitate – ask them to do the impossible!' the management urges. That includes bridge. **Cards:** *trefles*, *carreaux*, *coeur*, *piques*. Bonne chance!

KASBAH-BRIDGE

Card fanatics may have no wish to gaze out of the window, let alone go outside, but most prefer a passing glance to reveal traces of a foreign land. Think Kasbah Bab Ourika, a 50-minute drive from Marrakech. On one side, the hilltop building looks down on lemon and olive groves stretching towards the river; on the other, 'Arizona', a red rock escarpment backed up by the snow capped Atlas Mountains, makes a dramatic contrast.

Mine hosts, Claudia and Zebedee Stocken, have bridge in their genes. Father Peter is Andrew Robson's friend and one-time business partner; mother Dinah is a distinguished bridge-playing judge. Claudia does the meet and greet, Zeb deploys the bridge mastery. They're such consummate professionals that you may not want to leave them much time on their own.

SKI-BRIDGE

Trevor King's Alpine Bridge weeks in Champagny-en-Vanoise, near Les Arcs have become legendary since he introduced them in 1997. He picked the family-owned Hotel l'Ancolie for Frenchness, three-star ambience and swift gondola access into the Les Arcs–La Plagne axis. Baden Powell would have loved the man from Peterborough, leading from the front with Boy Scout impetuosity day and night. At 18.00, the resident Grand Master (GM), who plays for England, might give a lecture entitled 'Traps for the Unwary: Coping with Interference, Part 5'. Seems to be something about calling 2NT when opponents double partner's opening one-level bid in a suit bid. Seems to mean you'd have said something completely different if there'd been no double. The GM explains it smoothly, marking up explanatory hands on a white board. You try to focus, not to fidget, not too long for dinner, not to fear the duplicate that will follow. Only full bluffer alert will save you from revealing the extent of your incompetence. Your premonition is realistic: most of the guests are indifferent bridge players, but no way are they as bad as you. You come last. Your dreams are haunted: will you also be wearing the next day's funny hat for the person who falls most spectacularly on the snow?

Like the Polish cavalry battalions that charged German tanks when their country was invaded at the outbreak of the Second World War, bridge-skiers are insanely brave.

When you meet Trevor in the ski room after an early breakfast, he'll be dividing guests into groups according to ability and ambition. Someone young and gung-ho leads the wannabe racers. Trevor, who is not so young, but heroically fast, leads the chasing pack. The group releases in a tidal wave of exhilaration. Like the Polish cavalry battalions that charged German tanks when their country was invaded at the outbreak of the Second World War, bridge-skiers are insanely brave. Modest technique is the norm; survival slope craft means picking out those with no brakes. You'll ski in front of them at your peril. Spot the cavaliers: it may be better to avoid them at the bridge table as well.

As an averagely capable ski bluffer, you'll easily dodge the silly hat. Even before the coffee break, Trevor finds a long slope covered in icy moguls (big bumps in the snow). Within moments, the piste is covered in flying skis, cartwheeling bodies, boots pedalling thin air. Flame-haired Patsy takes the biscuit – and the hat – for bouncing off the tops of bumps like a rag doll for 100 metres before coming to rest at the bottom. As the party gropes for phones to call the blood wagon, she jumps up with a bright smile. 'Sun must be over the yard arm,' she cries. Once reunited with skis, sticks, hat, sunglasses, she straight lines it to the nearest bar.

As a lone bluffer you should join the holiday at St Pancras International at 09.45 on a Saturday. By the time you arrive, you'll have a pretty good idea of those you'd like to play with – and those you wouldn't.

Ski-bridge has the built-in merit of balancing intellect with exercise, but most other ski-bridge holidays lack the double-edged intensity of Alpine Bridge. In a small field, however, another stand-out is the Andrew Robson soft option variant which focuses on the four-star Hotel Alex in the well-established mountain resort of

Zermatt, in Switzerland. The bridge is relaxed rather than competitive. Before dinner, an hour and a half of tuition, instruction devised by Andrew, delivered by his faithful aide, Jack Stocken (brother of Claudia and Zebedee). After it, two hours of gentle duplicate or supervised rubber bridge.

SEA-BRIDGE

In no particular order, the advantages of cruising are only unpacking once, booze so cheap that it's included 24/7 in the basic price and being abroad but safely insulated from foreign parts when the ship drops anchor. The disadvantage is filling the time with meaningful thoughts when faced with endless ocean without suffering a cruise-length hangover. The travel company offers many fixes: deck quoits, a golf simulator, yoga and aqua-aerobics, lectures on archaeological sites and ancient monuments relevant to excursions it hopes to sell to passengers when the ship docks. And, of course, bridge.

This means a free trip for someone who's passed the Director's course, a four-day ordeal designed to display mastery of the EBU's much-thumbed slim yellow rule book. Successful candidates are entitled – begged – to be the guy who says, 'Move when you can please' or 'Enjoy your bridge' at club duplicate evenings. They are not begged to join cruises, but those with wangler's charm will scrabble aboard.

The certificate equips them to organise sessions rather than teach bridge, but a well-intentioned rookie Director might decide to slip in a lesson before getting the game under way. Wouldn't it be useful, he might think, to explain the different scoring implications in pairs and teams before giving the green light? No, it wouldn't. If the bluffer thinks he can get away with it he must cut this do-gooder off at the pass. A bidding box carelessly dropped on the floor, an unseemly struggle to scoop up cards and set them to rights should break the thread. A glance at your watch, an apologetic, 'Terribly sorry to hold you all up. Shall we get going now', might do the rest.

DON'T SAY: *'Have you ever tried underwater bridge? I can recommend it.'*

DO SAY: *'There is no rule stipulating that bridge has to be played on baize at a table for four. Indeed, the highest bridge session ever played (not including a plane) was on a sleeping bag close to the summit of K2 in the 1980s.'*

WHO'S WHO?

Those with careers that involve a lot of sitting around often take up bridge. Film stars and performing artistes waiting to be called; sportsmen stuck on the touchline, authors with writer's block, world leaders pausing on the red button, bluffers rehearsing a few fundamentals in a new area of professed expertise. Even them.

Chico Marx The eldest of five Marx Brothers was born Leonard, nicknamed Chicko for his 'chicken chasing' (womanising) and re-nicknamed Chico accidentally when a programme typesetter missed out the k. He was a compulsive gambler from the age of nine; as a New York City child, he'd pawn his parents' stuff to fund his habits; as an adult Marx Brother, he'd ask for expensive presents to be returned within hours of giving them so he could cash them in for stake money.

Bad habits sometimes had a silver lining. Chico's game of bridge with Irving Thalberg in 1933 prompted the hotshot Hollywood producer to sign up the Marx Brothers at MGM. Their more plot-driven collaborations,

A Night at the Opera and *A Day at the Races*, were smash hits; Groucho later claimed they were their best films. A year before his death in 1961, Chico made his last ever screen appearance in a high stakes rubber bridge game on the *Championship Bridge* TV show, hosted by pundit Charles Goran. As a reckless cavalier, Chico allowed America's captain, John Gerber, and his partner to win by a massive margin. Chico's verdict: 'It was a close match until the first hand.'

Omar Sharif Born in Alexandria as Michael Dimitri Chalhoub, son of a Lebanese rare woods merchant, in 1932. His film career was built on sultry Arabian glamour, but a degree in maths and physics from Cairo University and fluency in Arabic, English, French, Spanish and Italian equipped him for bridge domination whenever he took time out from hellraising with Lawrence of Arabia, aka Peter O'Toole.

He converted to Islam to marry his co-star on his first Egyptian film, but his on set affairs with Barbra Streisand (*Funny Girl*) and Catherine Deneuve (*Mayerling*) made juicy headlines. 'I realised afterwards that I couldn't have been in love', he said later, 'because it didn't hurt when the relationships finished.' There was no affair with Julie Christie during the filming of the worldwide hit *Doctor Zhivago*: he was repelled by her habit of eating fried egg sandwiches during breaks in filming.

His socialite mother, who entertained Egypt's King Farouk in their Cairo mansion, passed on her gambling addiction. With movie star money to burn, Sharif lost fortunes on horses, roulette, backgammon and bridge; the more he staked, the more he begged for ever more demeaning roles – third assassin, sleazy oriental gigolo – to raise the game. In the delinquent 1970s, he bought a spectacular £4.5 million house in Lanzarote from Sam Benady, the property developer who'd built it. He'd hardly moved in before he lost it. Bright bluffers know their enemies: as Sharif should have discovered, Benady was the reigning European bridge champion.

But the film star played on. 'Acting is my living, bridge is my passion. Many games provide fun, but bridge grips you. Your mind can rust you know, but bridge prevents the rust from forming.' Dementia caught up with him towards the end, but not until he'd celebrated Boris Schapiro's 90th birthday in 2000.

George Kaufman, playwright, director and founder member of The Round Table, the arts and letters gang who gathered daily for lunch at the Algonquin Hotel in New York from 1919 to 1939. Kaufman once announced, 'I'd rather be south than president.' On another occasion, he questioned a new partner who'd made an error. 'When did you learn bridge? I know it was yesterday, but what time yesterday?'

General Dwight Eisenhower didn't share Kaufman's views on the presidency. The Supreme Allied Commander in Europe during the D-Day landings and the onward march to Berlin served the full two terms after he was elected in 1952. His daily preparation for Operation Overlord – the invasion of Normandy – was 6 packs of cigarettes, 24 cups of coffee and as much bridge as he could squeeze in.

'You can always judge a man by the way he plays cards. Eisenhower is a calm and collected player who never whines at his losses. He is brilliant in victory, but never commits the bridge player's worst crime of gloating when he wins.'

Ely Culbertson, contract bridge champion

He learned to play at West Point in 1919. Accustomed as he was to calling shots, the only convention he allowed was Blackwood's (see page 53). No problem for Ely Culbertson: 'You can always judge a man by the way he plays cards. Eisenhower is a calm and collected player who never whines at his losses. He is brilliant in victory, but never commits the bridge player's worst crime of gloating when he wins.' The bluffer might suggest that this was the ideal temperament for navigating the ship of state through the chilly depths of the Cold War.

On Saturday nights, he hosted bridge at the White House with his favourite generals and celeb internationals like Ozzie Jacoby. Winston Churchill, keen but woefully amateur by comparison, was included on his regular visits. One clue to Ike's inner stress was his habit of raising his card high and thumping it down during play. Another was the way he yelled at his wife Mamie if he thought she'd made a mistake; she was equally addicted, but they rarely played together. No need to ask why.

Martina Navratilova 'No matter where I go, I can always make friends at the bridge table.' The Czech-born Aspen-dwelling tennis champion is a multiple grand slam winner. Her most memorable on-court victories were in singles, but she was equally skilled at doubles, a fine preparation for the game blame with your partner at the bridge table.

Blur In a four-man rock band, there's spare time to burn during recording breaks. Damon Albarn is an enthusiast, Alex James an obsessive. 'Bridge is utterly compulsive once it has got hold of you. It isn't too hard to learn and the joy is that you can play it and start enjoying it before you get very good. You can take it on at any level you want. The big problem is that very soon after you start you want to be brilliant.'

Radiohead In a five-man band, the maths is trickier, but Thom Yorke leads from the front, reading bridge columns and playing enthusiastically on tour.

Warren Buffett In a schedule packed with money and morality, the world's third richest man always finds time to play tournament bridge, often with Bill Gates as his partner. Is that enough? 'Bridge is such a sensational game that I wouldn't mind being in jail if I had three cellmates who were decent players and were willing to keep the game going 24 hours a day.' Doing time is unlikely for the 89-year-old uber investor, but felons should take heart.

'Bridge is such a sensational game that I wouldn't mind being in jail if I had three cellmates who were decent players and were willing to keep the game going 24 hours a day.'

Warren Buffett, uber-rich investor

Bill Gates The founder of Microsoft played bridge with his parents during his Seattle childhood, but getting together with Warren Buffett in the late 1990s turned a pastime into a passion. With all the money in the world, he hired double world champion Sharon Osberg to teach him and bought up a whole online store inventory to aid his learning curve. 'Bill does have an unusual thirst for knowledge,' said Fred Gitelman, founder of Bridge Base Online, wryly. Meanwhile, Gates has observed that, 'bridge is one of the last games in which the computer is not better'. He should know.

And ... 007: Keen card player, Ian Fleming, set up James Bond with a 7C doubled and redoubled contract against Hugo Drax, the evil billionaire in *Moonraker*. In

Blades, the London club based on Fleming's Boodles, M suspected Drax of systematic skulduggery at the tables. He was right of course. Whenever he dealt, the baddie used his highly polished cigarette case to reflect the cards. Playing with M, Bond substituted a rigged deck on the final hand to win £15,000.

Fleming borrowed the layout from the Duke of Cumberland who was set up with the same cards during a game of whist in the 19th century. Drax got off lightly compared to the son of George III. Convinced of the quality of his hand, the royal dupe bet £20,000 (an enormous sum in those days) that he'd win at least one trick. He didn't.

DO SAY: *'It was a close match until the first hand.'*
DON'T SAY: *'When did you learn bridge? I know it was yesterday, but what time yesterday?'*

There's no point in pretending that you know everything about bridge – nobody does – but if you've got this far and absorbed at least a modicum of the information and advice contained within these pages, then you will almost certainly know more than 99% of the rest of the human race about what bridge is, why it plays such a central role in many people's lives, why it can drive you mad, and how you can pretend to be better at it than you are.

What you now do with this information is up to you, but here's a suggestion: be confident about your new-found knowledge, see how far it takes you, but above all have fun using it. You are now a fully-fledged expert in the art of bluffing about the world's most cerebral and addictive card game. Perhaps it's the right time to take it up, but bear in mind that your life will never be as calm again.

GLOSSARY

Acol The British bidding system that took the bridge world by storm in the 1960s. Also the club in Hampstead where it was invented.

Baize Traditionally green, also blue, red and brown card table covering (invariably made from wool). A blank sheet until the cards come out.

Benji Acol The user-friendly version widely used in Brexit Britain.

Bidding box Basic tool of the trade. Finger it inappropriately and you'll face draconian penalties. Simply not done.

Board Oblong case or plastic wallet for dividing a pack of cards into four pre-dealt hands. Not essential, but desirable.

Bridgemate computer scoring device Often more enemy than friend as north keys in the scores for each board. At evening's end, the last button is pressed to reveal the overall results. Cue to crane forward – cheer or groan.

Brigista A player so submersed in the game that he kids himself, against all evidence to the contrary, that he's entitled to better partners, a higher ranking and a weekly spot at the top of the leader board.

Cheat seat The protected position. He who sits in it after three passes can relax the bidding rules and make a killing. Not to be confused with cheat sheet, a commercial crib beginners keep at hand to tell them what to do.

Chicago Short format scoring system, more sophisticated than rubber bridge. Popular with aspirational hostesses who claim to abhor gambling.

Convention card The display case for the conventions you claim, in hope more than conviction, that you can play. Unfortunately the card is more than a guideline: opponents can ask to see it and demand redress if you haven't followed it. For Luddites, the first stumbling block is editing the EBU (*see* below) pdf form, but there are many more to come.

Conventions The array of artificial bids on offer to help you come to the wrong conclusion. KISS – keep it simple, sucker – is excellent advice, but for most partners it's only foreplay.

Director The guy who takes control of the session, interrupting his own play to correct mistakes in yours. A suave and inscrutable smile covers bitterness at the pettiness of some interruptions or bafflement at the complexities of others. Free bridge on the night is scant compensation for soothing universal disgruntlement.

Double

Penalty double: 'You really think you can make that contract, sucker?'

Takeout double: 'Tell me something, partner, even if you haven't got it.' Expect blood on the baize.

Dummy Not the sap who allows wily opponents to tie him up in knots but the lucky guy who can go and buy a drink while all around him crash and burn.

Duplicate pairs The rolling competitive format favoured by players with horizons beyond the kitchen sink.

EBU (English Bridge Union) The ruling body and publisher of a rule book so arcane that it must have been written by a dysfunctional robot. The website is more user-friendly, though no money has been wasted on design. Likewise the other nations in the British Isles.

Fault Always theirs, never yours. Your confidence is more important than their discomfiture. Don't let it be dented.

Finesse A 50:50 play that often makes or breaks a contract. Bidding and inattentive opponents may improve declarer's odds, but expect the ruse to fail whenever it really matters. Ergo don't risk it if there's a better way.

Fourth suit forcing 'Must do' convention with six possible responses, most of them with scope for partner-apoplexy.

Handicap Automatic rating on the National Grading System (NGS) when you join a club. If yours is embarrassingly low, best have it removed from the listing on the EBU website. Let it stand and prospective partners can check you out before taking a chance on you. If you're under 50%, they may look elsewhere. In a spare moment, look up your regulars; the results will be entertaining.

Kitchen bridge No frills, lots of fun. Who needs stuffy conventions and silent reveries? Open the wine, deal the cards, get it done.

Luck

Bad: Opponents who make slams that no one else calls – a guaranteed zero for you.

Good: Scoring highly because opponents play badly – much more useful than it sounds.

Master points Rating points – local, blue and green – accumulated through finishing in the top third in qualifying competitions. The lowest is local master (less than 100), the highest Premier Grand Master (1,500 green points). In between, about 30 grades involving mastery and stars.

Nations On the World Bridge Federation (WBF) master points table, the strongest male players come from Poland, the Netherlands and the USA. And Monaco, but not by birth. For women, it's China, England and Sweden, followed by France and the USA.

No trump opener

Weak: 12–14 points, Britain's favoured method for opening the bidding with a lousy hand.

Strong: 15–17 or 18, the way the rest of the world asserts positive intent from the outset.

Orientation No prejudices please. Compass points divide pairs into north/south and east/west. North is the master commander in charge of pointing the boards in the correct direction and writing down the results. East dominates the horizontal pair, checking north's scoring at the end of each hand; south and west are the vassals.

Overcall The battle cry to compete in the auction after an opponent has opened.

Pack of cards They come in numbers divisible by four – *eg* 32 or 36 – but bridge requires the standard 52. With possible combinations numbering 8×10 to the power of 67 – that's 8 followed by 67 zeros – you'll never get the same hand twice. Unless there's a fix. ...

Parlour bridge The gracious version of kitchen bridge, hosted by ladies known for *savoir faire* and gourmet baking.

Partner A potential victim fated to be loved or loathed depending on the turn of the cards. When handled with care, transparency reduces stress: safer to solicit advice than insist on dishing it out.

Points Assess your hand by counting four for an ace, three for a king, two for a queen and one for a jack (totalling 40 points in a pack). With 12 or more, an opening bid is on the cards and you're on your way.

Psychic bid (verb **to psych out**). A grossly misleading bid designed to baffle partner and deceive opponents re the strength of your hand. Legal, but over-using will invite censure and penalties from embittered opponents.

Questions Queries allowed during bidding, followed by embarrassed silence when partner gets the answer wrong. To correct or not to correct? Wait until the auction finishes.

Revoke Playing another suit when you still have cards in the one that was led. No need to mention it if opponents don't notice – it's up to them, so this is not strictly cheating.

Robson, Andrew A degree in psychology and the uncanny ability to place and remember every card is the making of a legend. The self-styled 'tall correspondent' – 6ft 7in (204cm) – writes for *The Times* and teaches at his iconic Parsons Green club and nationwide with due compassion for lesser mortals. In between, he wins big tournaments, often in partnership with Tony Forrester, for a long time Britain's firebrand number two.

Ruff Playing a trump to take a trick when you're out of the relevant suit. Cause for hate, especially when it wins opponent's ace. Not to be confused with **French Ruff,** the English name for *Triomphe,* whist's 16th-century Gallic ancestor.

Sacrifice Bidding to lose less than opponents would gain by winning. A delicate calculation at the best of times, a yard sale at the worst. Partner will be ecstatic when it comes off. The reverse doesn't bear thinking about.

Signalling A legitimate but mind-blowing array of systems for exchanging lead requests with partner during play.

SIMS (simultaneous) Pairs Competitions in which players are graded with the others in regional groups as well as in their home clubs. Table money is doubled, with half going to charity.

Slam

Grand: Promising all 13 tricks can be bragger's heaven. Or not.

Small: Crow with caution. Making six is a good 'un until you realise everyone else has made seven.

Squeeze the pips out of a lemon. A declarer ruse for forcing opponents to discard potential winners as play progresses. When executed with artistry and advanced maths, he takes the last trick with the two of clubs.

Swiss pairs A form of match play where your opponents get tougher if you win, weaker if you lose. A Swiss characteristic? Ask Roger Federer. In *Bridge Fron Grunden* (Bridge from the Ground Up), Swedish author Erik Jennersten claimed the format for his native land, insisting that Swiss is Swedish shortened. Only the Swiss and Swedish are likely to care.

Teams Format favoured by players who'd like to take part in national and international competitions. Four, six or eight per team; expect selection problems at intro level – and probably ever after.

Tricks The building blocks of bridge. Win more, lose less is much easier said than done.

Trump The bid suit that has special privileges during play; surprisingly, it's not linked to the Donald.

Unauthorised information It's vital to conceal it until it's too late for opponents to expose and shame. Possession can be accidental, but not often. Cheating is another way of putting it. …

Vulnerability An emotional response to systematic bullying. Cry if you must but make sure your tears are crocodile.

Vulnerable The danger zone where penalties are punitively increased.

Weak jump overcall Not a show of fallibility or a suicide threat, but a device to warn partner he's on the brink. Terms must be agreed in advance.

Yarborough A hand with no card higher than a nine is laughable – unless it's yours.

A BIT MORE BLUFFING...

Available from all good bookshops

bluffers.com